SO-BDO-924

ABOUT THE AUTHOR

I.D. (Jim) James was born in Cambridge, New Zealand, and, apart from service in the Navy during World War II, has lived most of his life in the Waikato district where he currently resides with his wife, Rae, who is also very knowledgeable about orchids. He recently retired after 41 years in the Public Service.

Throughout his life this author has been actively involved in the promotion of orchids. A foundation member of the Waikato Orchid Society (1960), he has been both president and secretary of that organisation and was elected a life member in 1978. He has also been active in the New Zealand Orchid Society and the Orchid Council of New Zealand for many years and in 1983 his service was recognised by the presentation of the OCNZ John Easton Award.

At the Cymbidium Society Congress in Santa Barbara, California, Jim James was a guest speaker and he also addressed the International Orchid Show held in Auckland in 1980. He has participated in many local orchid seminars over the years, and has wide experience on judging panels both overseas and in New Zealand, where he is a Regional Registrar (OCNZ) and Reserve Judge (NZOS Inc.).

As an enthusiastic grower, Jim James has mastered the skill of mericloning and the flasking of his own seed pods, and many of his own seedling crosses have produced flowers of award standard. He has been generous with the knowledge he has acquired, visiting many orchid societies and giving numerous talks covering every aspect of orchid culture. His first book, *The New Zealand Orchid Grower*, was published in 1985. This latest handbook has been compiled to meet the demand for a beginner's guide to the basic culture of these increasingly popular plants.

BY THE SAME AUTHOR
The New Zealand Orchid Grower

THE
ORCHID GROWERS HANDBOOK

I.D. JAMES

BLANDFORD PRESS
London • New York • Sydney

First published in the UK 1988 by Blandford Press
Artillery House, Artillery Row, London SW1P 1RT

in association with
David Bateman Ltd, Auckland, New Zealand

Copyright © I.D. James 1988

Distributed in the United States by Sterling Publishing Co. Inc.,
2 Park Avenue, New York, NY 10016, USA

Distributed in Australia by
Capricorn Link (Australia) Pty Ltd,
P.O. Box 665, Lane Cove, NSW 2066, Australia

British Library Cataloguing in Publication Data
James, I.D.
  Orchid Growers Handbook,
  1. Orchids. Cultivation – Manuals
  I. Title
  635.9'3415

ISBN 0 7137 2066 2 (Hardback)
ISBN 0 7137 2069 7 (Paperback)

All rights reserved. No part of this book may be reproduced or transmitted in
any form or by any means, electronic or mechanical, including photocopying,
recording or any information storage and retrieval system, without permission
in writing from the Publisher.

Colour photographs — those opposite p. 33 supplied by the author; all others,
including those on the front cover, by Alan Patterson-Kane, Auckland
Line illustrations — those on pp. 36–7, 44, 46 by Agi Lehar-Graham; all others by
Gillian James

Typeset in Auckland, New Zealand, by Lazerprintz
Printed in Hong Kong by Colorcraft Ltd

CONTENTS

Comparettia

Chapter One

WHAT IS
AN ORCHID?

ORCHIDS IN THE WILD

The orchid family is one of the largest, if not the largest, in the plant kingdom. There are probably up to 25,000 different species growing in the wild. This means that of all the flowering plants on this planet, at least one in every 14 species must be an orchid. Forty-seven different species were once counted growing on just one tree in the rainforest in Venezuela. In considering how many different kinds of orchids there are, one must now add to these numbers the 60,000 or more artificial hybrids created by plant breeders — and even within a single hybrid population there is usually considerable variation among the individual plants.

Some orchids are found growing only in the ground. They are referred to as *terrestrials*. Others grow on trees and are referred to as *epiphytes*. *Lithophytes* grow on relatively bare rocks or cliff faces. In either of the latter cases the roots may be more or less exposed, giving a vital clue to cultural requirements. Many orchids which are regarded as terrestrial in cultivation grow, in nature, in the litter on top of the forest floor rather than in the soil itself. True terrestrial orchids are frequently difficult to keep alive if removed from their natural habitat. Epiphytes are less commonly found growing in the wild outside the tropics. Rich in epiphytes and other orchids are the mountainous (up to 3000 m above sea level) areas of tropical America and a wide area extending roughly northwards from Queensland up to the Himalayan foothills. Contrary to popular belief, hot steamy lowland jungles are not always rewarding places to search if one is looking for showy orchids.

THE FLOWER

The reproductive parts of other flowers typically comprise a central pistil with a receptive stigma surrounded by a number of stamens with anthers bearing pollen grains. In an orchid flower the stamens and pistils are usually partly or completely united to form a single structure called the *column*. This feature is unique — if the flower has it, it must be an orchid. Another distinctive feature is the pollen. Yellow and dust-like in most other flowers, in the orchid it is usually bound together in a few large masses called *pollinia*.

An orchid flower has three outer sepals (the parts visible when still an unopened bud) and three petals. One of the petals is usually modified to form a *lip* or *labellum*. In most of the orchids we grow for their floral beauty these flower parts are easily recognised for what they are. However, in many species they can be fused together or modified, often for the purpose of attracting, deceiving and manipulating insects to achieve pollination. This manipulation is to ensure the insect removes the pollinia only on leaving the flower, preventing self pollination.

As in other plant families, the flower attracts insects by colour and scent. Having arrived, the insect is then offered a reward. This is usually nectar but many orchid species offer quite different things, sometimes deceitfully. As an example, there are orchids where the flower must be pollinated by the male of a single kind of insect, usually a bee or a wasp. The flower attracts the male insect from a considerable distance by a scent which imitates that given off by the female insect. When the insect arrives it finds that the form of the flower so closely resembles the female insect that it is completely deceived. In its attentions the insect effectively transfers pollinia from one flower to another.

There are orchid flowers which are one-day wonders, lasting only 24 hours. Most of the kinds cultivated have long lasting flowers. There are orchids from high altitudes in New Guinea with flowers which persist for six months. Irrespective of how long a flower might otherwise remain open, it will probably quickly collapse once it is pollinated and its own pollinia is removed. Many a grower of cymbidiums has watched in horror as a bumble-bee flies past with pollinia attached to its back — somewhere in his or her collection, flowers in their prime could suffer an early demise. Happily most other kinds of orchids in cultivation, in the absence of the specific pollinator, are not too much troubled in this way by insects.

THE PLANT

To the uninitiated there may be nothing remarkable about an orchid plant not in flower and it could pass unnoticed. Nevertheless, there is such a diversity of size and form that it is difficult to select a typical plant to describe. As to size, few of us would wish to accommodate the massive *Grammatophyllum papuanum* with its 5-metre-long stems in our greenhouse. At the opposite end of the scale, a flowering plant of *Platystele jungermanniodes* might not cover a fingernail, despite its formidable name.

The growth patterns of different kinds of orchids fall into either one of two categories. *Monopodial* orchids have fleshy leaves on a single stem which grows upwards, in theory for ever. New roots and inflorescences are produced from nodes opposite the leaves. These plants usually do make a second growth to ensure survival of the plant if the terminal bud is destroyed. *Sympodial* orchids have a growth pattern more like most perennial garden plants. They make successive growths, each originating from the base of the preceding one to which they are connected, when mature, by a horizontal stem or rhizome. These growths do not develop further after they have matured and perhaps produced flowers.

Often the stem of a sympodial orchid is thickened into a cane or swollen in a bulbous fashion, when it is referred to as a *pseudobulb*. The leaves may be thin or may be fleshy and often persist for several years. When the leaves fall, pseudobulbs may remain alive for some years and these are referred to by growers as *backbulbs*. Orchids lacking pseudobulbs or thickened stems are usually not adapted to surviving for long periods without water. There are many technical terms to describe various types of inflorescences but whether there is one flower or many, the stem which bears them is usually called a flower *stem* or *spike* by orchid growers.

One of the peculiarities of orchids, particularly epiphytes, is that the roots are seldom thin and fibrous. They are often quite thick due to the presence of a spongy outer sheath of cells called the *velamen*. The velamen is white when dry but may be translucent or green when wet. Oddly enough, the tissue of the velamen is dead. However, its appearance indicates the health of the root. If the velamen rots, the life of the tissue below will be short.

ARE ORCHIDS EASY TO GROW?

If one gave any epiphytic orchid plant to a person who, not knowing what it was, planted it in the garden with, say, some cabbages, then the orchid would not survive. Such a person would declare that orchids are difficult to grow. On the other hand, if a cabbage plant was given to a person whose knowledge of plant cultivation was limited to epiphytic orchids and who tried to grow the cabbage in the same way, then the cabbage would die. That person would declare that cabbages were difficult to grow.

Orchids were certainly considered problem plants by the early growers in Europe over 100 years ago. In those times the plants often arrived in poor condition following long sea journeys, with many of them deteriorating further when grown much like cabbages but in the steamy hothouses the plants were thought to require. In those days reliable information as to where and how the plants were actually growing in nature was hard to obtain.

The modern orchid grower has the benefit of successful cultural rules and practices which have been worked out over many years. These rules are not hard to understand and apply. Most of the popular orchids can now be grown with no more or less difficulty than other pot plants. These popular orchids are usually ones prized for their unique floral beauty. There are, however, enthusiasts who spurn the modern hybrids and specialise in building up a collection of species, the rarer the plant or the more bizarre the flowers the better. These growers relish the challenge of species with unknown cultural requirements. A typical hobbyist will usually not be able to resist acquiring a few plants in this category. In general, some orchids are easier to grow for some people and in some environments than others. If you are new to orchid growing, try to either provide the conditions required by the plants you decide to grow, or otherwise specialise in those plants which will do well in the conditions and climate you already have.

CONSERVATION

The rainforests of the world are being destroyed at an alarming rate. The primitive slash and burn techniques employed in many tropical countries to obtain agricultural land are particularly devastating. When the forest is destroyed the orchid population dies with it. Bureaucracy, including an international convention (CITES) which is supposed to protect endangered plants, often effectively prohibits the collection and export of orchids from doomed forests or even from trees felled in milling operations. Some species of orchid, extinct in their native habitat, live on only in the greenhouses of the world. Thus the orchid grower has the opportunity to assist in the conservation of some of these species in the hope that some day it may be possible to re-establish them in their native habitat or a similar natural environment.

Although they may be relatively common plants, not all kinds of orchids have spectacular flowers. To one not familiar with them, most species would not be noticed as particularly remarkable plants and many citizens are quite unaware of the native orchid population in their own country. The species lacking current horticultural appeal are often the most endangered because fewer people care. Yet who knows what these species may have to contribute in the future?

Brassia

Chapter Two

ORCHID NAMES

NAMES ARE IMPORTANT

We know many garden plants by their popular or common names. However, we cannot always be certain other people understand us when we use these names. Plants can have several common names. Worse still, the same common name often refers to quite unrelated plants in different countries. Orchid growers only occasionally use common names (which orchids often do not have anyway) such as the moth orchid, the butterfly orchid, the dove orchid, etc. Even novice growers are quick to use the correct nomenclature. This is an important subject, not the least because even the way the name of, say, a hybrid orchid is written down, contains in effect a code which opens the door to a wealth of information about that plant.

GENUS AND SPECIES

The aim of plant nomenclature is to provide every kind of plant with an individual, internationally agreed name. Within the orchid family, closely related individual *species* (the word is both singular and plural) are grouped into *genera* (singular *genus*). Thus *Cymbidium* is a genus within which there are some fifty different species. *Cymbidium pumilum* is one of these. These two names together identify the plant. Note that both names are written in italics. From this alone we know that the plant is in fact a species and not a manmade hybrid. The generic name always begins with a capital letter and the names are in the Latin form.

Plants collected in the wild cannot tell us how they ought to be named. The classification system itself was devised by a human being and the dividing lines we have drawn between one genus or species and another can be blurred. From time to time modern knowledge suggests that a plant was not correctly classified when first discovered and name changes usually have to follow. On occasions it is found that a botanist described and named what he believed to be a new species unaware that it had already been named by somebody else, leaving a plant with two names. Where name changes have been proposed the reader is often assisted by being given both names. Thus we see *Cymbidium pumilum* (= *floribundum*) or *Cymbidium floribundum* (syn. *pumilum*). These name changes annoy orchid growers, who dislike having to alter familiar labels, but they must be accepted.

ORCHID HYBRIDS

It is stressed that we have been discussing only the naming of orchids collected in the wild. The naming of manmade or artificial hybrids is a different matter. Suppose we decide to make a hybrid between *Cymbidium pumilum* and *Cymbidium devonianum* following the procedure described in Chapter Nine. We may get a lot of seed and raise (if lucky enough to have the greenhouse space) say 1000 plants. These progeny are given a *collective* or *grex* name. In this case we would find that the hybrid has already been made and given the grex name Miss Muffet. Each one of our 1000 plants must be labelled Miss Muffet. There is still a problem, however, in that just as no two children of human parents look exactly alike (unless they are identical twins), neither do all the progeny of the two orchid parents exactly resemble each other. If the parents are themselves hybrids, the progeny, although bearing the imprint of the parents, may bear flowers varying from unappealing to exquisitely beautiful.

To identify one individual in a grex, it is given a *cultivar* name which is written down following the grex name. Thus in *Cymbidium* Miss Muffet 'Agate', *Cymbidium* is the genus, Miss Muffet is the grex and 'Agate' is the individual cultivar within the grex. Note that *Cymbidium* is still in italics. The grex and cultivar names are however in Roman print and usually in modern language rather than in Latin form. The cultivar name is enclosed in single quotation marks to distinguish it from the grex name. In a way grex names correspond to family (or surnames) and cultivar names to first (or Christian) names in humans. Thus the grex name of a clone really only tells us what the parents of that particular orchid were.

Yet that information will enable us to construct the complete family tree, as mentioned later. Growers will talk about crossing (i.e., hybridising) two plants and then commonly refer to the progeny collectively as a *cross* rather than a grex.

INTERGENERIC NAMES

Unlike many other plant families, the orchid family has groups of genera which interbreed with wild abandon. There are a few natural intergeneric hybrids but most are artificial — i.e., manmade. The question is what we do about the generic name for a hybrid between say an *Oncidium* and an *Odontoglossum*. The answer is that it is necessary to coin a new intergeneric name. In this case it would be an *Odontocidium*, a name which near enough to tells one what it is, but unfortunately this is not always so. Cross an *Odontocidium* with a *Brassia* and the trigeneric is a *Maclellanara*. Examples are *Odontocidium* Tiger Butter (*Onc. tigrinum* x *Odm.* Golden Avalanche) and *Maclellanara* Pagan Lovesong (*Odcdm.* Tiger Butter x *Brs. verrucosa*). Note that the intergeneric name remains in italics. When referring to parentage in this way, it is permissible to use standard abbreviations for generic and intergeneric names. Some of these abbreviations with some important generic and intergeneric names are listed at the end of the book — there are very many and nobody can memorise them all.

WHO CAN NAME?

Only a *taxonomist* (a botanist specialising in this field) is qualified to name or propose changes in the names of plant species. Any person may propose a grex name for a new orchid grex if he or she was the first person to flower a hybrid between one grex (or species) and another grex (or species). However, the cross and the name must be accepted for registration by the International Registration Authority for Orchid Hybrids in London. The Authority regularly publishes *Sanders List of Orchid Hybrids*. From this listing of grex names and parentages the family tree of any orchid hybrid can be constructed right back to the species.

A cultivar name can be given by any person. If that person does not possess the entire plant and propagations of it are held by others, they should be consulted. The cultivar name chosen must not be one used for any other cultivar in the particular grex. It is not usual to give an orchid the honour of a cultivar name unless the plant has some special merit. There is a nomenclature code which must be observed in choosing a name. If not familiar with it, ask someone who knows before attempting to name an orchid hybrid. Better still, *The Handbook on Orchid Nomenclature and Registration*, published by the International Orchid Commission, will tell you all you should know.

AWARDS

Many national orchid societies have judging systems which give recognition to orchids of outstanding merit. In descending order of excellence, First Class Certificate (FCC), Award of Merit (AM), and Highly Commended Certificate (HCC) are the awards most often seen. With some societies gold, silver and bronze awards or medals are the equivalent. An awarded cultivar has abbreviated award details written down following the name. Thus *Sophrolaeliocattleya* Madge Fordyce 'Red Orb' AM/AOS and *Cymbidium* Jubilation 'Geronimo' FCC/AOC were awarded by the American Orchid Society and the Australian Orchid Council respectively. *Cymbidium* Citation 'Pastel Queen' B/CSA was awarded a bronze medal by the Cymbidium Society of America.

PRONUNCIATION

Even if you did not study Latin when at school, do not be deterred from using botanical names. Be encouraged by the fact that there is no agreement as to the way in which many names ought to be pronounced. For example speaking of the genus *Laelia*, various people will say 'LEE-lee-a, LIE-lee-ah' or 'LAY-lee-a' and may quote scholarly authorities to support their different pronunciations. If in doubt, pronounce the name the way it looks or the way others do. Someone who professes to be more knowledgeable may correct you, but you will almost always be understood.

Angraecum

Chapter Three

ACQUIRING PLANTS

QUALITIES TO SEEK

A good plant is one which is free from disease and has the genetic ability to grow strongly under average cultural conditions. A poor plant might just be worth the trouble of growing if at its best it is capable of bearing flowers of exceptional quality. Defining a good orchid flower is not easy, and beauty, as always, is in the eye of the beholder. If a flower appears beautiful to you, the opinions of others do not necessarily matter. However, it is a fact that there is an innate perception of beauty in an orchid flower which varies little among experienced people around the world. Orchid judges usually agree on the following:

Broad flat sepals and petals with rounded ends rather than thin narrow or twisted ones with pointed ends.

Wide rather than narrow lips.

Bright colours (including crystal clear white) appeal more than dull colours which may be acceptable if texture is glistening.

Size of flower or inflorescence should be large in relation to plant size.

Stems should lift flowers clear of foliage. Flowers should look at you rather than nod or point to the sky.

The above points are a guide only. Some kinds of orchids are not inherently structured to possess all these attributes, yet are still beautiful.

One outstanding factor, such as colour, may lift an orchid to greatness even if it is deficient in some of the other qualities. In general, if a plant is in flower when acquired, you can see what you are getting in terms of flower quality. There can be both rewards and disappointments in acquiring plants not in flower. These will be dealt with next.

LARGE PLANTS

Flowering size plants offered for sale are occasionally culls discarded by a grower for some reason, perhaps because they were seedlings which did not flower up to expectations. Plants in the latter category should be approached with caution if they are not in flower. However, they are often offered cheaply and if well established and healthy, could be a good buy for a beginner.

Large plants of most genera can be divided into pieces and these propagations will of course all have identical flowers. The price of these propagations or *divisions* as they are usually called, is influenced by the flower quality and rarity. Divisions of high quality, recently awarded cultivars can be expensive. In many genera there are older hybrids of high quality available. Divisions of these can be acquired inexpensively, mainly because they have been extensively propagated over the years and have no rarity value. Buying a mature established plant means one can expect it to flower again in its next flowering season. A plant that can be removed from its pot by a gentle tug is not established in that pot. Beware of any large plant which has no remnants of old flower spikes — if the vendor could not flower it, you may not be able to either.

UNFLOWERED SEEDLINGS

In nature, orchids grow in association with a root fungus. This relationship (called *mycorrhizal*) assists the nutrition of the plant. Most importantly, orchid seeds germinate in the wild only if they have been infected with the correct fungus. If orchid seed, which is very minute and often dust-like, is scattered on the top of a pot it may be that the right fungus is present and very occasionally a few seedlings may appear. Just after World War I a formula was developed which would germinate seed readily in a sterile flask. This method for mass propagation helped to reduce the price of orchid hybrids and it was soon no longer only the wealthy who could enjoy growing them. Buying unflowered seedlings is still one of the least expensive ways of building up an orchid collection.

There are bewildering numbers of unflowered seedlings on the market. Selecting these can be both a problem and a fascinating exercise. As explained in Chapter Two, no two seedlings from the same seed pod are likely to have flowers which look exactly alike. There have been a very few crosses made over the years in which almost every seedling was an award winner. Typically, a cross will produce a range of flowers varying from those with breathtaking beauty to utter rubbish. Raising seedlings is a little like backing a racehorse. Although a gamble, you can choose what to put your money on. The excitement of watching the flower of a new seedling about to open just has to be experienced to be understood. Often it will be disappointing. The occasional outstanding flower brings great joy to the owner and, human nature being what it is, the collector's glow of satisfaction in knowing that nobody else has that particular cultivar.

Seedlings from the same seed pod may vary not only in flower and plant form but also in vigour. The slower growers are likely to be still struggling for survival years after their more vigorous brethren have flowered. The more vigorous seedlings frequently produce the finest flowers. The fastest growing 10 per cent of a cross are worth paying several times more per plant for than the run-of-the-mill ones — if the owner is willing to sell them. At the other end of the scale, the runts in a cross may be near to worthless. There have, however, been some quite famous exceptions to this, so one can never be sure.

In general, the price of the seedlings will be governed by the size of the plant, the reputation of the hybridiser, the quality and reputation of the parents as stud plants, and the results of any similar matings in the past. The cheapest way to buy seedlings is in sterile flasks. Further, if bought in flasks there is rather less likelihood that they will have been picked over before you get them. There will be a long wait for flowers, perhaps two to seven years depending upon the genus and the skill of the grower. Some skill is necessary in caring for seedlings to ensure their survival during the critical few months following their removal from the sterile flask, but do not let this deter you from trying them. Instructions for deflasking plants are given in Chapter Nine.

TISSUE CULTURE

In the 1960s a technique was developed which resulted in the successful culture and proliferation, in a sterile flask, of a tiny piece of undifferentiated or meristematic tissue taken from a bud or shoot of an orchid. The process can be continued until the required number, whether hundreds or thousands, of plants has been produced. The name *mericlone* has been coined to describe a plant propagated in this way. In theory each mericlone, being in effect a vegetative propagation, should be a replica of the original plant. In practice there are occasional variations, not always desirable, including reduction in plant vigour, and virus diseases can be transmitted to the mericlones. Despite some disappointments, mericlones offer the opportunity of assembling a collection of quality plants at a modest cost. Modest, that is, compared with the thousands of dollars at which many plants of equivalent quality changed hands prior to the 1960s.

Mericlones usually cost somewhat more than seedlings of the same plant size. This reflects the extra work required to produce them and often the royalties being paid to the owner of the original plant. The cost is influenced by the quality of the original plant and tends to reduce as the number of mericlones increases. Mericlones are sometimes offered for sale in sterile flasks. They will look like seedlings and the procedures for deflasking and subsequent care are the same. Unfortunately some genera have not yet fully yielded to the tissue culture process.

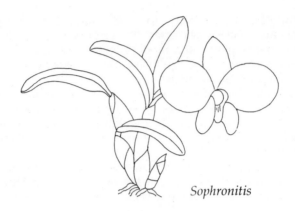

Sophronitis

Chapter Four

THE GROWING ENVIRONMENT

LIGHT

Plants with green leaves need the energy in sunlight to function and grow. Orchids will make the best growth if given the optimum intensity of light from sunrise to sunset. However, this optimum is less than unobstructed sunlight for most kinds grown in temperate latitudes, especially in summer. Some shading is usually necessary, heavier for some genera than others. Light heats solid objects, including plants. In summer, orchids may have to be given light intensities lower than they require just to keep leaf and flower temperatures from rising too high. Subject to this, it is better when in doubt to give too much rather than too little light. Excessive light intensities will result in leaves showing more yellowness than they should. However, deep green leaves, although normal for orchids with low light requirements, may indicate insufficient light intensity for plants needing brighter light.

The foot-candle is a well known light unit and can be measured with a light-meter. The shadow cast by a hand held 30 cm above a leaf is a useful rough guide. If the shadow has sharply defined edges, the light could be over 5000 foot-candles. If the form of the hand can be distinguished but the edges are blurred, there is probably over 2000 foot-candles. If a shadow can be detected but there is no outline to suggest what is causing it, then light is likely to be under 1500 foot-candles. Bear in mind that light intensities can vary throughout the day. They will be higher in those times and places in a greenhouse where the sun is at a right angle to the plane of the glass, shadecloth or other sheathing material and lower where the sunlight enters at an acute angle.

TEMPERATURE

Warm growing orchids typically like day temperatures of about 30°C (86°F) falling to 20°C (68°F) at night. Day and night temperatures for cool orchids are usually quoted at 20°C (68°F) and 10°C (50°F) respectively. These temperatures are a guide only and with many genera may be allowed to drop lower at night if certain precautions are taken. All orchids require some drop in temperature at night time and some will not flower without it. Many high-altitude orchids described as cool growing seem to be in that category only because they do not like very warm day temperatures.

The temperatures quoted above (and in all orchid literature) are air temperatures measured by a thermometer hung in a well ventilated area but in the shade. If the sun is allowed to fall on the thermometer, the readings will be meaningless. The maximum temperature an orchid will tolerate is largely determined by leaf rather than air temperature. It can be judged by holding the leaf. If it is cool, all is well. If the leaf is warm, conditions may be tolerable but if it is relatively hot to the touch, the plant could be under stress. Heat can build up to alarming levels in orchids with thick leaves. These can actually burn unless shade and/or air movement is increased. Temperatures are usually higher inside a greenhouse than they are outside during daylight hours. Keeping greenhouse temperatures down during sunny summer days can be a problem for the orchid grower.

HUMIDITY

Humidity has to do with the amount of water vapour in the air. The warmer the air, the more water it can hold and vice versa. When air of a particular temperature is holding say one half of the water vapour it is capable of holding at that temperature, the *relative humidity* is said to be 50 per cent, or 75 per cent if three-quarters the amount, and so on. If it is holding all it is capable of, the relative humidity is 100 per cent, that is, the air is saturated. The air in a greenhouse at dawn is often near saturation point. As the temperature rises with the sun, the air must take up the extra moisture it is then capable of holding to keep the relative humidity at 100 per cent. It can rarely do this unaided, so the relative humidity drops as the day progresses and temperatures rise. It may drop too low for the welfare of the plants on a bright, hot day unless we do

19

something to get more water in the air. Orchids prefer relative humidities of between 50 per cent and 90 per cent and will suffer, some genera more than others, if the figure is below 30 per cent for long periods.

The relative humidity can be raised by watering the greenhouse paths, benches and walls, a procedure referred to by orchid growers for over a century as *damping down*. Better are fine mists or sprays of water under the benches or where they will not water the plant pots. If air from outside the greenhouse is blown through such a spray, there will be dual benefits. Not only will there be more evaporation to raise the humidity but because evaporating air absorbs energy, the air will be cooled. This is known as *evaporative cooling*. On the other side of the coin, high humidities may not be beneficial on cold winter nights. As the temperature falls after sunset, some of the water the air is holding appears as condensation inside the roof and walls of the greenhouse. If the temperature falls too far too quickly, the air may not be able to get rid of the water fast enough on these surfaces. A dew may then appear on the plants and, as discussed later, this may not be desirable.

Relative humidity can be accurately measured with a wet and dry bulb thermometer. This is an inexpensive instrument, but cumbersome to use. Hygrometers with direct reading dials are available. The cheaper ones are not very accurate but can still be useful indicators.

AIR

Orchids definitely respond to air movement around them. Good air circulation helps to ensure that the right concentrations of oxygen and carbon dioxide are at the leaf surface. This is important even at night time as some orchids take in carbon dioxide only during the hours of darkness. Air movement is necessary to help keep leaves cool during hot days. In general, if the air is humid and at an equitable temperature, the stronger the movement the better. On the other hand, strong draughts of very cold or very dry air will do more harm than good, so some discretion must be exercised. There is nothing like good air movement to dry up dampness on the plants and prevent diseases from becoming established.

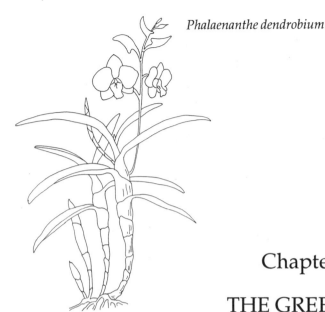

Phalaenanthe dendrobium

Chapter Five

THE GREENHOUSE

BASIC FUNCTIONS

Any closed-in structure in which the grower can create the climate required by the plant is a *greenhouse*. A *shadehouse* is a structure covered with shading material, usually shadecloth of some form, giving plants the degree of shade they require plus some wind protection but allowing little control over temperature or unwanted rainfall. These structures are sometimes called *lath houses* or *bush houses* — depending upon the materials of construction. A shadehouse nevertheless can provide satisfactory and relatively inexpensive housing for a range of orchids in areas where the temperature does not fall below freezing point.

A shadehouse or a greenhouse can utilise one wall of an existing building and becomes a *conservatory* if one can enter it from one's home. In fact any sunporch or other glassed-in area in a home can be adapted to become an orchid house. Such structures are best sited on a more or less north-facing wall (facing south in the Northern Hemisphere). A wall facing away from the sun will not receive enough light in winter. Even a free-standing greenhouse should not be unduly shaded by trees or buildings. These may provide welcome shade in summer but will cast very long cold shadows in winter.

FRAMING MATERIALS

Timber will almost certainly be the first choice if you are building the greenhouse yourself from the raw materials. It is the traditional material for framing glasshouses and is satisfactory if a durable timber is used. If treated with preservatives, timber should be painted to prevent these leaching out and possibly poisoning the plants. Steel makes a strong frame but unless it is galvanised it is difficult to keep rust at bay in the moist interior of a greenhouse. Aluminium is virtually maintenance free and the first choice for a small glasshouse. It is also the most expensive. Aluminium glasshouses sold in kitset form should need little more than a spanner and a screwdriver to assemble or to dismantle if they have to be relocated.

SHEATHING MATERIALS

Glass is the traditional material and many claim (whether correctly or not is debatable) that the best orchids are grown under it. Glass lasts forever (or until broken) and shading paint can be applied and removed without damaging the surface. Framing costs may be higher as glass has to be installed to more exacting standards. There are now so many materials which can be used instead of glass that it is impossible to review them all. Those that come as plastic films usually only last from one to three years. However, they provide relatively cheap and easily fixed covering for a rough framework or temporary cover over a shadehouse. The various rigid plastics can make an airtight and watertight house and tend to be replacing glass. The best of them are claimed to be long lasting (how long is still uncertain) and although often costing more than glass, money can be saved with a lighter and simpler supporting structure.

Plastic films are particularly suitable for fixing inside an existing greenhouse to give a double-glazed or twin-skinned effect. The still air pocket then enclosed forms a thermal insulation barrier which will keep the interior warmer in cold weather and/or reduce heating costs. Plastic films will last longer here than when exposed to direct sunlight. Because the inner skin will be warmer, there will be less condensation on it but the possibility of some on the plants. Such a house will tend to have higher humidities at times and as these are not always beneficial, extra attention to ventilation is needed. On the subject of insulation, do not build or buy a greenhouse which admits light right down to ground level. We do not grow orchids down there. Unwanted light coming in under the benches will only help to raise day temperatures in summer and allow more heat to escape on cold winter nights. An orchid house is best constructed on a cement or brick base up to bench height or a little lower.

SHADING AND VENTILATION

As already discussed, shading may have to be increased during hot summer months just to keep temperatures down. It is accordingly desirable to be able to vary the intensity of the shading from time to time. Glass can be painted with one of the white (it should never be coloured) shading mixtures on the market. These should ideally be persistent enough to withstand summer rain yet be able to be removed with a light brushing. As good as any is a mixture of 1 part (or less) of white acrylic house paint to 10 parts of water. To this must be added enough whiting to make a slurry of cream-like consistency. Whiting is finely ground calcium carbonate, sometimes sold as precipitated chalk. Do not use even diluted acrylic paint on its own, as it may be very difficult to remove.

The best shading (from the point of view of the orchid) is undoubtedly that provided by shadecloth suspended outside the roof and a little above it. A popular system in days of old was to use timber slats in a roller blind which could be rolled up and down. Less flexible but easier to install is shadecloth suspended inside the greenhouse. However, although this shades the plants, the greenhouse will be warmer in sunlight than if the shadecloth is suspended on the outside. In the latter case the unwanted light, and hence the unwanted heat, does not enter the greenhouse. If the greenhouse is sheathed in a plastic or glass substitute which cannot be safely painted then there is no simple alternative to using shadecloth or some similar arrangement.

Ventilation is linked with shading to the extent that a good air flow keeping plants cool may reduce the amount of shading required. The usual arrangement is to have some ventilators low down below the level of the plants and others as high up the roof as possible. Convection, helped by wind pressure, results in an air flow through the bottom and out the top of the structure. An extractor fan will give control over air flow. It is best installed in the end wall of a greenhouse with ventilators at the other end. Air is then pulled along the length of the house. Many orchid hobbyists grow excellent plants without any fan-assisted ventilation. In general, heat builds up more quickly to higher levels, other things being equal, in very small greenhouses and ventilation is more of a problem with these than in larger structures.

STAGING

Attempts to cultivate terrestrials and semi-terrestrials such as cymbidiums in beds at ground level have not been very successful. Orchids are best kept off the ground on benches. A good bench height for a mixed collection is about 75 cm. Half that height is better for cymbidiums and other larger plants. Galvanised iron mesh is increasing in popularity as a surface on which to stage plants. It is hygienic, allowing water to drain quickly through it, and allows good air movement up through the plants. Slugs and snails have difficulty traversing wire mesh.

HEATING

A wide range of orchids can be grown in an unheated greenhouse in areas where the temperatures do not fall much below freezing point. In marginal localities it is good to have some portable device for emergencies. Even sheets of newspaper placed over the plants will provide a surprising amount of protection. Flowers may be spotted by fungal organisms in an unheated greenhouse when temperatures are low and humidity high. In a small, unheated collection, plants in flower will last longer at these times if brought inside your home. If the local climate and the minimum temperatures needed by the kinds of orchids being grown require the greenhouse to be heated, attention should be given to heat losses. Making sure there are no leaks where warm air can escape, and reducing radiation and convection losses by double glazing (e.g. twin-skinning), will reduce fuel costs dramatically.

The heating system will depend upon the kind of fuel chosen. We have seen a small greenhouse heated by decomposing lawn clippings, and a large area heated by burning biogas (methane) produced from organic material in an anaerobic digester. More practicable fuels are:

Coal Used to heat water which is circulated in pipes or by air blown over radiators. The cheapest fuel in some areas but inconvenient and capital cost high. More suited to large installations.

Oil Used to heat water as with coal but more amenable to automation. Not so popular now that oil is no longer a cheap fuel.

Kerosene (paraffin) Mainly used in small portable heaters which can be relatively cheap to buy. Best kept for emergencies. If not burning cleanly, the fumes may damage flowers and possibly plants.

Natural Gas Worth considering if local cost is cheaper than electricity. Combustion fumes should be vented to the exterior of the greenhouse as these may contain toxic gases.

Electricity The first choice for a small greenhouse if convenience and low capital cost are the only considerations. A fan heater can be controlled by a thermostat and/or a time clock or other devices giving a degree of automation. Having electricity in the greenhouse permits the use of lighting, hot beds, pumps and much more.

WINDOWSILL CULTURE

Orchids can be successfully grown and flowered in the home on windowsills. Colombian miltonias grew better for the author in an east-facing bathroom window than they did in his greenhouse. The trick seems to be to get the right kind of orchid for the particular window and room temperatures. We hesitate to recommend particular plants but in general avoid trying to grow orchids with high light requirements or those which grow into very large plants. A window facing north (south in the Northern Hemisphere) is preferable, but do provide the necessary degree of shading with suitable curtains. Members of the *Cattleya* alliance are popular choices for this position but there are many possibilities. For a window facing more to the east or west try an orchid with lower light requirements. *Phalaenopsis* and *Paphiopedilum* hybrids are among those which are being grown here. The relative humidity in a home is usually on the low side for orchids and it is common practice to stand the plants over (not in) a tray of water. The pots must not touch the water. Lowland tropical orchids will of course require the room to be maintained above the minimum temperature they will tolerate.

Equitant oncidium

Chapter Six

MEDIA
AND NUTRITION

GENERAL REQUIREMENTS

The ideal *medium* (or compost) in which to grow orchids is one which has a high air capacity, a high amount of easily available water (these two requirements being often contradictory), the ability to provide nutrients for the plant, and one to which the roots like to attach themselves. Provided the air capacity is high and the medium is not actually toxic, orchids will often survive in almost any medium. The air capacity or air-filled pore space can be roughly measured by filling a full container of growing medium with water. If then allowed to drain, the water which drains out will equate the volume of air now in the growing medium. This should ideally be not less than 30 per cent of the total volume of the growing medium for epiphytes (much more for some) and probably well over 15 per cent for terrestrials.

MEDIA RECIPES

Fern fibre from various *Osmunda* species used to be the universal material for potting orchids. It is now difficult and expensive to obtain in most places in the world. Coarser fibre from the roots and trunks of various kinds of tree ferns may be used if available. Some of this material seems to contain a growth inhibitor when fresh and should be well weathered before use. Supply difficulties have now turned most orchid growers to other materials. The list of what has been tried alone or in combination is almost endless but includes sawdust, bark, charcoal, peat, ricehulls, scoria, pumice, sand, rockwool, turf roots, coconut fibre, sphagnum moss and various plastics. A salient feature of most of these substances is that they are either inert or slow to decompose. Most substantially retain their form over the two or more years they are expected to support the orchid. Organic materials which break down quickly can decompose epiphytic orchid roots at almost the same speed.

Pine bark used by itself is probably the most popular growing medium for orchids at the present time. It can be used in the form it is purchased but is likely to benefit from some pre-treatment. Bark from different tree species will have different properties, but all or some of the following treatments are often recommended:

1. Unless dust free, screen out the dust and very fine particles.

2. Put through further screens to obtain the particle size required.

3. Many barks including those from Douglas fir (*Pseudotsuga menziesii*), red fir (*Abies magnifica*), white fir (*Abies concolor*) and *Pinus radiata*, are very acidic. Orchids will benefit from the addition to these of up to 3 kilograms of dolomite lime per cubic metre. While doing this it is worthwhile adding single superphosphate (in powder form) at the rate of 1 kilogram per cubic metre.

4. Fresh bark can contain toxic substances. Storage in a moist heap for 2 to 6 weeks will help remove these. Do not store on soil (unless the bark is to be sterilised before use) as it may become infected with disease organisms.

Orchid growers tend to experiment with mixes in a search for the perfect one for their conditions and this is to be commended. Hundreds of recipes for growing media (some containing as many as nine different ingredients, excluding nutrients) have been published. It is not proposed to attempt to review them all here. Below are details of a selection of different media. We have given them all names so they can be easily referred to when discussing the culture of various orchids later in this book. The bark in the mixes should preferably be treated as above unless it is known to be from a tree species with non-acidic bark.

Fine bark Particle sizes of 2 mm to 4 mm. This will have an air capacity of about 40 per cent.

Coarse bark All particle sizes of 4 mm to 10 mm included. This will have an air capacity of over 50 per cent.

Mix for cattleyas If the medium below dries out too rapidly, reduce the polystyrene content. The polystyrene spherules are about 5 mm in diameter and are sold for packing or for bean bags.

Coarse bark	7
Polystyrene spherules	2
Shredded sphagnum moss	1
Total parts by volume	10

Mix for cymbidiums To each cubic metre of the mix below should be added 3 kilograms of dolomite lime and 1 kilogram superphosphate inclusive of any previously added to the bark.

Fine bark	4
Pumice (2 to 4 mm)	2
Sphagnum moss peat	3
Total parts by volume	9

Sphagnum moss Shredded or unshredded, alive or dead (but not decayed), this is an amazing growing medium. Used on its own, it seems capable of growing a wide range of orchids, especially small seedlings, and reviving many which have lost their roots or are otherwise declining in other media. This notwithstanding that to the uninitiated sphagnum moss seems not to possess all the qualities we believe that a successful medium ought to have. It is longlasting but prone to growths of algae on the surface, especially if kept moist and supplied with nutrients. It must be a good quality product, such as New Zealand sphagnum moss.

NUTRITION

Like other plants, orchids need food. The main elements taken in by the roots are nitrogen, phosphorus and potassium. Plants also need some calcium, magnesium and sulphur plus a number of others (micro-elements) in very minute quantities. The relatively inert growing media typically used does not in itself provide enough nutrients for good growth so the grower must provide these. Nutrients in organic form (such as blood and bone, chicken manure, etc) need to be acted upon by organisms in the medium before nutrients are released in a form available to the plant. Most inert growing media do not support a very high population of suitable soil organisms. If organics are applied and do succeed in working up the organisms into a population explosion, these are liable to break down the growing medium as well. For this reason the modern practice is to supply nutrients in inorganic form as mineral salts.

If, when potting, we put into the growing medium in soluble form the total amount of nutrients likely to be required by the plant for the two years or more it is expected to be in the pot, there will be trouble. The first watering will dissolve so much material and the solution will be so saline that the roots will be destroyed. By the time any new roots appear much of the soluble material will have leached out. The orchid must accordingly be provided with a constant supply of nutrients at the correct strength. There are two ways of doing this. The first is to use one of the proprietary brands of slow-release fertilisers. The most popular of these contain all the necessary nutrients in soluble form but in granules coated with a special resin. The nutrients escape only as required and when the plant is watered. The manufacturer indicates how long the they will last, which may be up to nine months. This method does not give the grower complete knowledge or control over what is happening but is convenient and safe if applied in the recommended amounts. It is useful for plants not often hand watered — e.g., those exposed to rain in a shadehouse.

The second approach is to put soluble nutrients in the water supply. This gets the best results if done at every watering. Ten times the amount of nutrients every tenth watering may damage the roots of the plants. There are many proprietary formulations on the market designed for liquid feeding. The proportion of nitrogen (chemical symbol N), phosphorus (chemical symbol P) and potassium (chemical symbol K) is usually indicated. Thus a product with an NPK of 20:20:20 would be expected to contain 20 per cent each of nitrogen, phosphorus and potassium. The remaining 40 per cent could include some other elements required by the plant. Trace elements are in any case usually added. Unfortunately there are two ways of stating NPK ratios, the older one being to express P and K as oxides of these elements. Thus a product with a stated NPK of 20:20:20 originating from the USA is likely to actually have 20 per cent N but only 9 per cent P and 16 per cent K in elemental form.

One proprietary product with a 20:9:16 NPK ratio (20:20:20 USA) when diluted at the rate of 0.5 grams per litre (0.08 oz per gallon) provides about 100 parts per million nitrogen and is a good general-purpose ratio for orchids. Some heavy feeders such as cymbidiums in bark (which has an appetite for nitrogen) may need a higher nitrogen ratio. In general follow the manufacturers' instructions as to dilution but with caution if a strength several times the example above is suggested. Plants can take in nutrients through their leaves and orchids may respond to this foliar feeding. Do not rely entirely upon it. Formulations specifically designed for foliar feeding are not always recommended for application to the roots of plants not growing in soil. Some proprietary products which seem to rely more on auxins, hormones and unspecified growth substances rather than their NPK content often appear to be beneficial if applied occasionally as an addition to, not a substitute for, a solid NPK diet. Resist any temptation to sprinkle dry mineral salts on top of the pot — it might work if followed by very heavy watering but is very risky.

The grower can make up a liquid feed to suit his or her own requirements, usually at a considerable saving in expense. In the suggested formulas below, based on three salts, the quantities are in grams per 200 litres:

	N50 P7.5 K50	N100 P15 K50	N170 P37.5 K150
Ammonium nitrate	16	42	55
Monoammonium phosphate	6	12	30
Potassium nitrate	26	26	79

As an example, adding to every 200 litres watered on to the plants 42 grams ammonium nitrate, 12 grams monoammonium phosphate and 26 grams of potassium nitrate provides N, P and K at a dilution of 100, 15 and 50 parts per million respectively. An occasional watering with magnesium sulphate (Epsom salts) at the rate of 40 grams per 200 litres will provide magnesium. You do not have to make up 200 litres at a time. It is permissible to dissolve the above quantities of salts in say 2 litres of water and then dilute this concentrated stock solution at the rate of 1 in 100 for application to the plants. Be cautious about applying any other trace elements as the risk of toxic effects of excess will be more serious than a deficiency. The occasional application of a proprietary product containing trace elements should be sufficient.

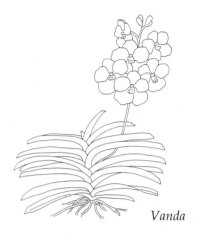

Vanda

Chapter Seven

WATERING AND POTTING

WATERING

If, following watering, the roots of an epiphyte or lithophyte are still water soaked a week later, there could be problems. We may get away with it occasionally, such as when an unexpectedly long spell of cold, sunless weather follows a watering, but if it happens regularly many kinds of orchids will lose their roots. Some plants must at least approach dryness at the roots within a day or two of watering. The period of time taken for roots to dry out will be governed by humidity, intensity of sunlight, day length, air movement, temperature, the nature of the growing medium and the kind of pot. If one is having difficulty getting a short drying cycle, it may be that potting techniques need adjusting. This cycle will be shortened by reducing the pot size, reducing the amount of growing medium in the pot, by changing from plastic to clay (earthenware) pots, or by changing to a growing medium which dries out more quickly.

Great emphasis has been placed on watering because experience has shown that faulty practices have caused more plants to go into a decline than any other factor. Having said this, it must be stressed that there are orchids which do not like to be quite dried out between waterings and even a few, including most terrestrials, which like to remain quite damp.

These will be identified when they are described later in the book. The best advice we have heard for the beginner is that if in doubt about whether an epiphytic orchid should be watered, don't, but if in doubt about a terrestrial, water.

Water quality is often blamed without justification for orchid troubles. If your public water supply is not very good for growing pot plants this fact is likely to be generally known in your area. A simple test is to water a few plants with rainwater collected in a plastic container. This must not be collected from a roof coated with any toxic material such as the anti-corrosive paints often applied to iron roofs. If after two to three months your rainwater plants are looking perceptibly better and greener than the others, the normal water supply must come under suspicion.

CONTAINERS

Orchids can be grown in containers of many kinds. Clay (i.e., earthenware or terracotta) pots were once in general use but plastic containers are now more popular. Some plastics become brittle after a few years in the sun and plastic containers cannot be heat sterilised — see Chapter Eight. On the credit side, they are cheaper, lighter, and if black in colour, will be warmer in sunlight which promotes growth with many orchids. Clay pots are still preferred for some genera and because they dry more quickly are safer for the beginner to use.

The drainage hole or holes in a pot must be covered in such a way as to prevent fine material blocking them. Pieces of broken clay pots (often referred to as *crocks*) are favoured, but irregularly shaped expanded polystyrene is suitable. Often the pot is one-third or one-half filled with crocks. This may not improve drainage but reduces the volume of the growing medium proper, quickening the drying cycle. An epiphyte in a very large pot often suffers from too frequent waterings because although it may be dry on the surface, the middle of the pot can remain wet. It is a good idea to place an inverted small pot at the bottom of such a pot (ensure that the drainage hole is not blocked) to provide an air space to this central zone. A piece of expanded polystyrene is even better. It should extend from the bottom and up the middle of the pot almost to the plant rhizome.

An epiphyte or lithophyte sends its roots over the surface of the tree branch or rock in nature. One side of the root is more or less exposed to the air. Placing such a plant in a position where its roots are covered and growing around the inside of a pot is not natural. A few orchids (to be discussed in later chapters) resent this because their roots require a very short drying cycle and/or do not like being disturbed, or just do not like being covered. These orchids can often be successfully cultivated on slabs

1. **Laeliocattleya Puppy Love 'True Beauty'** HCC/AOS (*Cattleya* Dubiosa x *Laelia anceps*)

2

3

4

2. **Cattleya Irene Holguin 'Spring Glory'** (Astral Beauty x J.A. Carbone)

3. **Cattleya Milton Warne 'Dream Girl'** (Hybrida x Suavior)

4. **Laelia kautskyana** — a fine Brazilian species

5. **Cymbidium Cherry Blossom 'Profusion'** (*pumilum* x *erythrostylum*) — an unusual miniature

6. **Cymbidium (Tom Thumb x Claudona)** — a miniature hybrid of *Cym. pumilum* ancestry yet to be named

7. **Cymbidium Parish Jewel** (*parishii* x Miss Muffet). The pendulous spike is inherited from a *Cym. devonianum* ancestor.

9

8. **Cymbidium Glad Rags 'Party Time'**
   (Doris Aurea x *tracyanum*)

9. **Cymbidium Citation 'Pastel Queen'**
   B/CSA (Dorama x Wallara)

10. **Cymbidium Touchstone 'Mahogany'**
    (*devonianum* x Mission Bay)

8

10

12

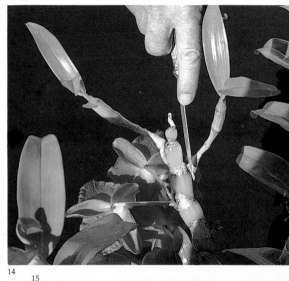

14

15

11

13

16

POTTING AND PROPAGATION

11. Due largely to poor culture, this *Cymbidium* is mostly back bulbs. The solitary flower spike has just been removed. It has outgrown the container but if potted on to a larger one will continue to look rundown and will not produce good quality flowers. A plant which looks like this is best broken up.

12. When broken up, the *Cymbidium* yielded three green-bulbed divisions which should develop into strong plants. The dark root colour suggests these are old and suspect — many decayed roots had already been removed before the picture was taken. The divisions will establish more quickly if potted in quite small containers. The 9 back bulbs can be encouraged to shoot and make new plants (see Chapter Eleven) but will take two to four years to reach flowering size.

13. The knife blade indicates where the rhizome of this *Cattleya* was severed four months previously. This has resulted in the older and previously dormant part of the plant on the left making a new vegetative shoot. Each division may now be potted up separately. Cutting the rhizome can be delayed until immediately prior to dividing but the back division may then not establish so quickly, or even survive.

14. The top two nodes on the cane of this *Dendrobium nobile* hybrid produced adventitious growths instead of flowers, probably encouraged by inappropriate culture. However, roots are just emerging from the base of these so they can be removed and potted up to make new plants.

15. Plants removed from flasks, unless very large, will usually make better growth if crowded together quite closely in community pots. Clockwise from the left are seedlings of *Sarcochilus, Odontoglossum, Sophronitis* and *Cattleya*. At this critical stage, plants should be inspected frequently for any early signs of disease.

16. Some potting media described in Chapter Six are shown. Clockwise from top left: fine bark, coarse bark, mix for cymbidiums, mix for cattleyas. In each case the bark is from *Pinus radiata*.

of well weathered tree-fern fibre, cork or bark. For the latter, part of a tree branch which is already supporting lichen and mosses should be chosen, but find out from other growers what local trees in your area have been used successfully. Secure the plant to the slab with nylon thread. Some orchids (e.g., *Vanda* and *Phalaenopsis*) like to have a few roots in the growing medium and the rest waving around in the air. These are commonly grown in baskets.

REPOTTING

Most orchids are at their best when the plant completely fills the container. Do not move a plant to a larger pot until it is absolutely necessary. When it must be done select another pot just large enough to accommodate the plant for two years, no longer. Orchids will sulk if moved to a pot which is too large. If in doubt, choose the smaller size. Remove the plant from its old pot as best you can. Healthy roots are bound to suffer some damage in the process and this must be accepted. If the roots are in fact healthy and the old growing medium has not broken down, the complete root ball is sometimes just positioned in the new pot and new medium placed around it. Otherwise, or if there is any doubt at all, it is preferable to remove all the old medium together with any dead roots. In that case ensure that the roots are spread out against the inside wall of the new pot and work the new medium into the middle. Never push the new medium down the sides of the pot forcing all the existing roots into the middle. Sympodial orchids should be positioned with the oldest parts of the plant against the side of the new pot so that the new growths have a space to grow into.

For each kind of orchid there seems to be an optimum pot size. If the container is very much larger than that, the plant will often not do as well. When that stage is reached, or when the grower does not find it convenient to handle a large pot, the plant must be divided into smaller pieces. This is discussed later when considering the propagation of various kinds of orchids. Whether dividing (often referred to as *breaking up*) or merely repotting a plant, the best time is when new roots are just appearing. If the plant is in bud most growers will prefer to delay repotting so the flowers may be enjoyed even if this results in problems later on. An orchid should be repotted at any time if the growing medium has broken down and all the roots have died. Even under the most favourable conditions an orchid will suffer some shock on being repotted. It should be placed in a shady position and watered sparingly until it has recovered.

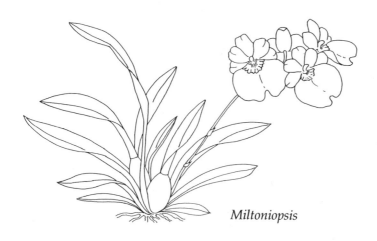

Miltoniopsis

Chapter Eight

PESTS AND DISEASES

PESTS

Many ordinary garden pests can attack orchids. Some of these prefer certain kinds of orchids and are rarely a problem with others. The list which follows includes some of those more commonly encountered. A selection from the many agricultural chemicals available for treating specific pests is given but bear in mind that some of these are marketed under different names in various localities. Orthene and Kelthane are trade names for acephate and dicofol respectively. Malathion and Omite are trade names for maldison and propagite.

Two-spotted mite The adult is about 0.5 mm in length, straw coloured (it may be reddish), and a hand lens will show the two characteristic black spots on each side of the body. It is found on the underside of the leaf and is usually more of a problem for orchids with thin leaves. A silvering of the leaf surface is often the first indication of its presence. These mites proliferate rapidly in a hot, dry atmosphere. They dislike water, high humidity and low temperatures. To control, spray underneath the leaf surface with Omite or Kelthane. Give a repeat spray ten days later. Having selected an effective spray, keep with it and

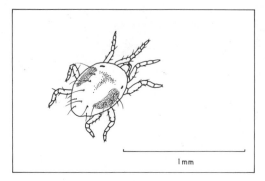

Two-spotted mite
(*Tetranychus urticae*)

l mm

change to another only when the mites develop a resistance to it. Never give the mites a shotgun mixture of all the chemicals claimed to kill them — you may breed a strain resistant to the lot and be left with nothing to control them.

Other mites   Several other kinds of mites can become established, frequently on the top surface of the leaf. These can be very tiny, a powerful hand lens being required to see them. Malathion or Diazinon will usually give control if the sprays suggested for the two-spotted mite are not effective.

Aphids   A large aphid population will often build up unnoticed in the greenhouse. They favour flowers and tender new growths. Orthene is popular with orchid growers, but aphids will succumb to a wide range of insecticides.

Scale insects   Persistent spraying (i.e., over several weeks) with Malathion, Diazinon or Orthene will control these. The young mobile stages are easy to kill, the adults with their waxy covering more difficult. If you have just a few plants, wiping the leaves with summer oil (be careful to follow directions) will give immediate results.

Mealybug   These pinkish sluggish insects appear white due to surrounding white cotton-like filaments. Some possess what appears to be a long white tail. Like aphids, they can secrete honeydew which grows a black, sooty mould. Spray with Malathion, or Diazinon or Orthene, especially in crevices and in the axil of new growths where they hide. Incorporate a fungicide in the spray if directing it into leaf axils where it may not dry quickly.

36

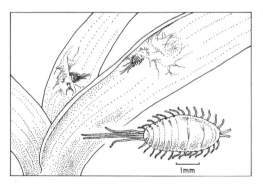

Mealybug (*Pseudococcus longispinus*)

Large insects The foregoing pests all suck the sap of the plants. Chewing insects which eat leaves and flowers can be tracked down individually but spraying with the materials suggested for aphids and scale will eliminate most. Some insects may be predators and thus allies, but treat any unidentified insect with suspicion.

Slugs and snails Apart from the obvious advice of preventing them from gaining entry to the greenhouse, metaldehyde or Mesurol baits offer the only conventional control. Watch out for a tiny snail which hides in the growing medium and which pits roots and nibbles their growing tips. Many a beginner has seen this damage without knowing the cause. One has to go out at night time to catch them in the act.

FUNGI AND BACTERIA

These can spread through infected water splashing from plant to plant or through the air by spores which may germinate if they land on a damp surface. Do not allow stagnant water to remain on leaves, particularly in

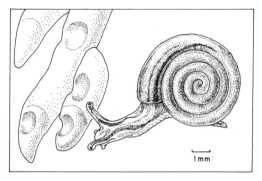

Orchid snail (*Zonitoides arboreus*)

the crown of the plant. Do not let a dew form on leaves, especially in cold weather. Good movement of dry air will prevent many problems. A bewildering array of fungicides and bacteriacides are available. There are modern fungicides which can easily eliminate some diseases yet be ineffective against others, or even encourage them. For this reason they are not always useful unless the problem is first accurately diagnosed. Among the chemical controls favoured by orchid growers are Benlate (benomyl), Captan, Dithane M45 (mancozeb), Terrazole (etradiazole), Physan and Natriphene. Benlate and Terrazole are systemic, that is, they move into the plant and attack infection from within. The others can only form a protective external coating to provide a barrier which the disease organisms cannot penetrate or get established on. These protective materials are not always effective after the disease organism has gained entry to the plant.

The average grower is often unable to see, let alone identify, the specific fungi or bacteria involved, or even to be sure that the symptoms are caused by these organisms. Bearing this in mind, one approach is to group symptoms into the three categories below.

Leaf-spotting fungi These cause various spots and blemishes on the foliage. They seldom kill a plant and are often more unsightly than lethal unless they cause loss of foliage. Spraying periodically with Captan or Dithane M45 should prevent these organisms gaining a foothold. If flowers are getting spotted, chemicals are not much help, or at the best will leave unsightly residues on the blooms. The answer is to increase air movement and lower relative humidity. In a small collection, plants prone to this trouble can be brought inside the home while they are in flower.

Root rots As discussed previously, these arise from faulty growing, particularly watering practices. However, disease organisms are usually present in the final stages. Often leaves and pseudobulbs are shrivelled. Remove the plant from the pot and dip it in a solution of Natriphene or Physan after removing decayed roots and repot with new potting mix in a clean pot. If other plants are considered to be at risk but still have some live roots, drenching with a mixture of Terrazole and Benlate (these are active against different groups of organisms) may help. Do not use Benlate unless necessary as some fungi can build up a resistance to it. With epiphytes, keeping the growing medium dry for an extended period may help to check disease organisms.

Rots More serious than mere leaf-spotting organisms are those causing water-soaked black or brown areas which continue to enlarge at an alarming rate and threaten to engulf the entire plant. Some will be checked in the early stages by swabbing with Physan or Natriphene. If the rot continues to spread, cut out the diseased areas and drench the whole plant in Terrazole and Benlate. One drenching of Terrazole can give protection for several weeks against *Pythium* and *Phytophtora*. These fungi spread through water. Water stored in open tanks (e.g. rainwater) in which leaves and other debris can collect are a sure source of infection. Maintaining a protective coating of Dithane M45 or Captan on the leaves will prevent some of these organisms getting established. Do not allow leaves to remain wet for long periods.

VIRUS

Viruses are entities that can multiply in living cells yet are too small to be seen with any light microscope. Symptoms in the foliage of an infected plant include yellowish or dark streaks, blotches or mottling often with sunken leaf surfaces and occasionally in a mosaic or diamond-shaped pattern. Flowers may be streaked with brown, white or more intense coloured markings. Plant growth may be stunted. The same virus may cause different symptoms in different kinds of orchids or the plant may show no symptoms at all. The difficulty for the grower is that diagnosis by symptoms alone is not always reliable. Symptoms similar to those mentioned can be caused by fungi and bacteria and many other things. In general if a plant which has always had clean green leaves starts consistently producing leaves with virus like markings which do not appear on other neighbouring orchids or respond to spray programmes it should be placed under suspicion. There is no cure at present and infected plants would be a source of infection for others if not isolated or destroyed.

Virus in orchids just might be transmitted by sap sucking insects but the grower usually spreads it when handling plants. It pays to wash the hands thoroughly after dividing or repotting a plant and before handling another one. Always sterilise a knife (by heating to a cherry red) before using it on another plant, even if only cutting off apparently dead flowers. Pots and stakes must be sterilised before re-use for a different plant. Clay pots can be heated (and knives too) in an oven for one hour at 180°C (350°F). Plastic pots are more of a problem but after they are cleaned thoroughly they can be soaked in a chlorine containing solution such as household bleach (sodium hypochlorite). As a final word on virus, examine carefully any new plant brought into the collection. As virus is not supposed to be transmitted by seed, seedlings produced in a sterile flask should be virus free. Mericlones in flasks will probably be infected if the mother plant was.

OTHER AILMENTS

Occasionally symptoms resembling virus, fungal or bacterial infections are not caused by any actual disease organism. A few, not all mentioned elsewhere in this book, are:

Charcoal It will be toxic if made from timber treated with preservatives.

Creosote Timber impregnated with this will give off volatile substances which can damage plants in an enclosed structure.

Engine exhausts Do not use any internal combustion engine in a greenhouse. Even orchids at the side of a shadehouse where vehicles passed frequently did not thrive.

Failure to flower If the plant is mature and growing vigorously and has never flowered, this may be an inherited trait. Try more light, no nitrogenous fertiliser and dry out for extended periods.

Light Excessive light may cause purple pigmentation on susceptible plants. Strong light coming through a gap in the shading or through a ventilator can burn orchid leaves. The most sinister looking lesions can form on orchids with thick leaves.

Treated timber See Chapter Five. Using timber treated with preservatives to make rafts and containers must be risky.

Water As suggested earlier, the rainwater test can be tried on orchids but they can often be slow to recover from a setback. If water must be stored, plastic tanks are best. Water stored in galvanised tanks or reticulated through new galvanised iron piping can cause zinc toxicity which shows up in stunted growth and straw-coloured leaves.

HORTICULTURAL CHEMICALS

It is difficult to grow fine orchids without resorting to the assistance of chemicals at least occasionally. The degree of hazard they present to the grower can vary from virtually harmless to those which are deadly poisons. None of those mentioned earlier in this chapter is in the latter category. However, although all should be treated with respect, one should not be afraid to use them. Provided the instructions on the label are followed especially as to gloves, protective clothing and face protection if stipulated, you are unlikely to harm yourself or anyone else. Be especially careful handling the undiluted material.

Plants can be damaged by normally safe sprays if they are applied incorrectly. Use at the recommended strength and do not spray plants twice merely to avoid wasting material still in the spray tank. Do not spray plants under any stress (e.g. because watering was overdue) or spray in bright sunlight or very hot days. On the other hand, bear in mind that insects are cold-blooded creatures and are most active in warmer weather and the more active they are, the more effective the spraying will be. Early in the morning on a warm cloudy day is best, but ensure that the spray will be dry before nightfall. Use spray as soon as it is mixed. Manufacturers seldom date their material and as some formulations deteriorate with age, buy them from a source that is turning over stock quickly. It may be false economy to buy more material than you would use in two years.

Masdevallia

Chapter Nine

ORCHIDS FROM SEED

HISTORY

The first manmade orchid hybrid was flowered in 1856. It created something of a sensation at a time when the suggestion that plants could be mated to produce hybrid offspring was beyond the comprehension of many horticulturists of the day. It was, however, not long before an increasing number of growers were attempting it. Although they could produce seed, it was difficult to germinate, and orchid hybrids in quantity did not become available until this problem was overcome in the early 1920s. With the coming of the mericlone in the 1960s, interest in seedlings waned somewhat. Many people preferred to purchase what were in effect vegetative divisions of plants of known quality rather than gamble on getting something good out of a batch of seedlings.

Commercial growers in some countries do not now find the growing of seedlings for sale much beyond the flask stage to be always economically viable. There is still a strong demand for seedlings of exceptional promise, sired by very superior parents, and for seedlings of genera which cannot yet be reliably propagated by tissue culture. Against this background the amateur grower is becoming more and more involved in orchid hybridisation. Unlike the commercial grower who has reputation and financial return to consider, the amateur is free to indulge his or her fancy in unlikely crosses where the odds against success are high but the potential for rewards great. The excitement of the imminent first flowering of a seedling has already been mentioned in Chapter Three. This excitement is unbounded if the seedling is one you yourself have hybridised and raised. Those growing orchids as a hobby are encouraged to try their hand at hybridising and the remainder of the chapter is devoted to this and the raising of seedlings.

CHOOSING THE PARENTS

A well tried formula recommended to the beginner is to merely cross one superior orchid with another of equivalent quality. Crossing two inferior orchids is likely to produce more of the same. An otherwise inferior flower which possesses one desirable characteristic, say colour, will occasionally combine well with another which has all the other qualities it lacks. With no more knowledge than this you can try your hand at plant breeding. If you wish to go into it a little further, consider the following:

Study other crosses Some crosses have produced more than their share of award winning cultivars. Find out the parents of these crosses, and their ancestry generally. *Sanders List of Orchid Hybrids* (see Chapter Two) will help. You may be able to follow the more successful and proven breeding lines.

Stud plants From the foregoing you will not be surprised to learn that there are in most genera cultivars that have a reputation for siring good offspring even when the other parent is mediocre. These proven stud plants used to be difficult and very expensive to obtain but many are now available as mericlones.

Laws of inheritance The simple laws discovered by Gregor Mendel over 100 years ago are described in many botanical books and the serious hybridiser should be guided by them. Much knowledge has been accumulated about inheritance in various kinds of orchids but unfortunately nobody has yet attempted to document it all in one book — one just has to study the literature.

Colour This one characteristic is singled out for special mention as it holds traps for the unwary. Purple tends to be a dominant colour in the orchid family. There are many exceptions, but more often than not all the progeny will have flowers with some purple or lavender pigment if only one of the parents has it. Avoid such flowers if you wish to breed clear yellows, reds, greens or whites and are not certain you are dealing with one of the exceptions to the rule.

Reciprocal crosses There is evidence to show that there can be differences in two populations of seedlings where the roles of the parents as pollen donor and seed bearer are reversed. Make the cross both ways if you can. It is not uncommon to find a species or hybrid which will refuse to set a seed pod but which has quite fertile pollen — or vice versa.

Avoid the impossible You could make history by flowering a hybrid between a *Cattleya* and a *Cymbidium*. However, there is really no chance of doing this by natural means. Hybrids are usually only possible between plants which are already much more closely related than the two genera mentioned. Attempts to cross flowers of greatly different size usually fail even if they are related.

TETRAPLOIDS

The hereditary material of an organism is ordered into chromosomes. These normally exist in two paired sets in the nucleus of each cell. Cattleyas and cymbidiums each have two sets of 20 chromosomes, a total

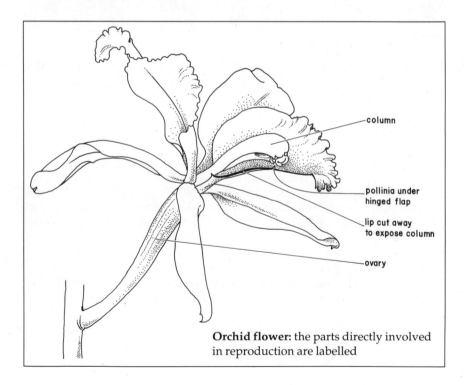

column

pollinia under
hinged flap

lip cut away
to expose column

ovary

Orchid flower: the parts directly involved in reproduction are labelled

of 40. Other kinds of orchids may have different chromosome numbers. There are now many cultivated orchids which have four sets or double their normal number of chromosomes, and are referred to as *tetraploids*. This doubling sometimes happens by chance in the flask stage and can be induced deliberately in the laboratory in some cases. Tetraploids tend to have heavier and larger flowers with wider petals. They are also slower growers and have other disadvantages. Nevertheless, many of the superior modern hybrids are tetraploids, and for this reason are heavily favoured as stud plants. If a tetraploid is crossed with a tetraploid each parent will contribute two of its four chromosome sets to the progeny which will thus be tetraploids also.

TRIPLOIDS

If a tetraploid is crossed with a normal diploid plant the progeny will be *triploids* with three sets of chromosomes in each cell. Two of these will have been contributed by the tetraploid parent and one by the diploid. As all or nearly all of the characteristics of the individual are dictated by the genetic code in its chromosomes, it could be expected that triploid progeny will tend to look more like the parent supplying two thirds of its chromosomes. In fact tetraploids are very dominant when mated with a diploid and the plant breeder needs to take this into consideration. Triploids are usually sterile, or at the best do not produce much useful seed if used as a parent. Orchid literature often uses the symbols 2n, 3n and 4n to refer to diploid, triploid and tetraploid states respectively.

MAKING THE CROSS

Having chosen the parent plants, the next step is to prepare the flower which is to bear the seed pod. Flowers which are nearing the end of their life or which are just opening are not good subjects. Operate when the flower is about one-third through its life, that is, when a flower which will normally last six weeks has been open for two weeks. Remove its pollinia and throw it away unless you are going to use it on another flower. (It can be stored for some weeks in clean notepaper in a domestic refrigerator.) Remove the pollinia from the flower which is to be the male parent and examine it to make sure it is in good condition and not mouldy. Good pollen is usually waxy and bright yellow in colour, but may be pale or with a few orchids hard and black. Place all the pollen on the sticky stigmatic surface under the column of the flower to bear the pod. You then wait.

Within hours or a few days there will be a change in the pollinated flower. Usually, but not in some genera, the flower parts will collapse and die. If all is well the ovary will begin to swell and form the fruit or seed capsule of the orchid. This is commonly called the *seed pod*. The pod will take six weeks to six months or even longer to mature. Ripening is indicated by the pod yellowing and eventually splitting open and spilling out the seed. It should obviously be harvested before this happens.

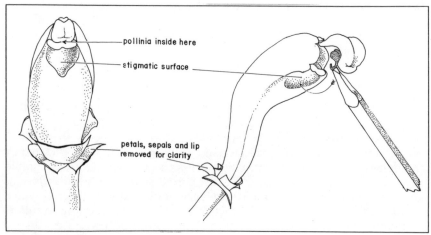

Pollinating an orchid using a sharpened matchstick

Each kind of orchid has its own particular period of gestation. If the pod yellows or is infected by disease before this period has elapsed, the seed is usually not viable. Orchid seed is minute and a pod can hold several million seeds. A low-power microscope will reveal a dark embryo in fertile seed. Fertile seed is typically cream or yellowish in colour. Snow-white seed is usually infertile.

SEED SOWING

Unfortunately many modern complex hybrids are reluctant to produce seed. The flower can so affronted at being pollinated that it immediately dies and drops off the plant. More often a pod will start to develop but will abort long before there is any hope of viable seed. One should keep trying and not be discouraged by these failures.

Having succeeded in producing what is hoped will be viable seed, you can send your creation to one of the many laboratories which will sow the seed for you for a reasonable fee. If the seed is viable, you will receive the seedlings in sterile flasks some six to 18 months later. Enquire first whether the laboratory requires a green pod or unripened pod or the harvested dry seed. Green-pod sowing involves sterilising the outside of the pod so that the seed inside can go straight into the flask without further treatment. Otherwise the seed itself must be sterilised, which involves some risk. If dry seed is to be harvested, do it yourself as soon as the pod has started to change colour but before it bursts open. Seed can be stored in folded notepaper (never plastic) and placed in a cardboard box in the vegetable compartment of the refrigerator.

The preparation of the culture medium, sterilisation and seed sowing is commonly regarded as a laboratory procedure. However, it does not have to be and many enthusiasts successfully handle a few flasks in the kitchen or bathroom with a minimum of special equipment. A description of the formulas and procedures is beyond the scope of this book but can be found in specialist literature. As an alternative, one can try using a host plant as did the growers of old in the hope that the right mycorrhizal fungus is present to invade the seed and permit germination. Select an adult established plant of the same or closely related genus and scatter the seed on the surface of the pot. Do not bury it. The plant is then best watered when necessary by immersing it nearly to the top of the growing medium so as not to disturb the seeds. The method only occasionally works and it may take many weeks before any results are evident. Growers who have done it successfully report that the few seedlings obtained usually grow with exceptional vigour.

DEFLASKING

Seedlings need a lot of help if they are to survive the shock of having to face the real world outside the sterile flask in which they were raised. A piece of wire with a hook bent at the end is a useful tool with which to remove plants from a flask with a narrow neck. Drag the seedlings out roots first. Adding a little warm water and shaking the flask gently will loosen the plants from the agar jelly. If the plants are too big to remove in this way without damage, wrap the flask in a towel and break with a hammer. After removal, any jelly remaining on the plants (and glass splinters!) should be washed off with warm water. Add a fungicide such as Captan to the water. The seedlings can then be planted out in regular growing medium. This should ideally be first sterilised. Better still, try shredded sphagnum moss. Unless the plants are very large, resist the temptation to plant them out in individual pots. They like company and get away better if crowded together in a community pot so that they are almost touching each other. Do not bury them — only the roots should be in the growing medium.

The newly planted seedlings should initially not be subjected to more than half the light intensity recommended for adult plants. They should be kept warm but protected from heat stress and given as much humidity as possible. A plastic bag or inverted glass jar placed over a community pot will help to keep up the humidity. Water with discretion and do not give any nutrients until there is some sign of new growth. At this stage the young seedlings are prone to infection by disease organisms. Spray them regularly with a preventative fungicide such as Captan or Dithane M45. The water moulds *Pythium* and *Phytophtora* can be particularly devastating. A precautionary drenching with Terrazole will provide protection. If a single diseased plant is noticed, it is best removed immediately. Once the plants are growing strongly, they can be treated like adult plants but should not be exposed to excessive light levels.

17

17. **Dendrobium** (Joanna Mesina x *bigibbum*)

18. **Dendrobium Bardo Rose** (*falcorostrum* x *kingianum*)

19. **Dendrobium Jamie Upton** (*tetragonum* x Golden Fleck)

19

18

21

20. **Odontonia Papageno** (Anglaon x *Miltonia vexillaria*)
21. **Vuylstekeara Howard Liebman 'Frolic'** (*Odontioda* Shelley x *Miltoniopsis* Athene)
22. **Odontoglossum Stonehurst Yellow** (Many Waters x Golden Guinea)

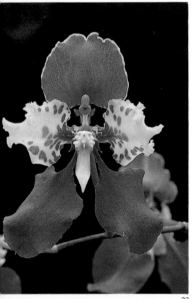

22

23. **Oncidium 'Geyser Goldmine'** (*macranthum* x *chrysodipterum*)
24. **Miltoniopsis Gascogne 'Vienne'** (Emotion x Lady Veitch)
25. **Oncidium** (Eye Popper x Celebrity)

20

23

24 25

26

28

26. **Paphiopedilum insigne**
27. **Paphiopedilum hybrid**
28. **Paphiopedilum Saint Swithin 'Wellington'** AM/OCNZ (*philippinense* x *rothschildianum*)
29. **Phalaenopsis** (In The Pink x Lippeglut)
30. **Phalaenopsis Yukimai** (Musashino x Grace Palm)

27

29

30

31

32

32. **Sophrolaelia Marriottiana** (*Laelia flava* x *Sophronitis coccinea*)

33. **Lycaste Koolena 'June'** HCC/OCNZ (Koolena x Koolena)

34. **Sarcochilus** (Lois x Fitzhart)

31. **Zygopetalum Artur Elle** (Blackii x B.C. White)

35. Display by Tauranga Orchid Society

33

34

35

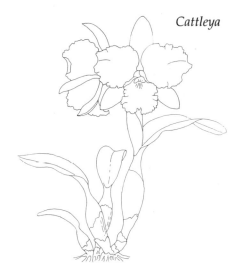

Cattleya

Chapter Ten

CATTLEYAS

HISTORY

The first *Cattleya* species was flowered in England in 1824, a genus that was until then unknown to science. The story is told how a horticulturist, Mr William Cattley, rescued and eventually flowered the plant from a consignment of lichens and mosses shipped from Brazil in 1818. The *Cattleya* had been used as packing material. It was named *Cattleya labiata* in honour of the grower, and the flamboyant beauty of the flower created something of a sensation at the time. Cattleyas of the *labiata* type did not reach Europe in large quantities until the latter half of the nineteenth century. By the end of the century they were not only common in cultivation but they had become the flower that most people would be likely to recognise as being an orchid. They were the orchids found in expensive corsages. They were the flower used by anyone who wanted an illustration of an orchid for anything from postcards to chocolate boxes.

There are over 40 other genera which are so closely related to cattleyas that most interbreed readily and there is now a vast assemblage of these intergeneric hybrids. Growers talking about cattleyas are often loosely referring to the whole alliance. The cultural suggestions in this chapter are intended to refer to them all except where otherwise indicated. The other genera most widely cultivated or used in hybridisation are *Brassavola, Broughtonia, Encyclia, Epidendrum, Laelia* and *Sophronitis*. The

49

names of the more common intergeneric hybrids are listed at the end of this book. *Laeliocattleya* (*Laelia* x *Cattleya*), *Brassolaeliocattleya* (*Brassovola* x *Laelia* x *Cattleya*) and *Sophrolaeliocattleya* (*Sophronitis* x *Laelia* x *Cattleya*) are some almost always found in general collections of cattleyas.

The relative popularity of cattleyas in the florist trade has declined since World War ll due to the competition from other genera, including some moved around the world by airfreight. On the other hand, enthusiasm for these flowers among hobbyist growers remains unabated, and you will find them cultivated everywhere from shadehouses in the tropics to greenhouses covered in winter snow in cooler climates. This enthusiasm is fuelled by intense hybridisation which is continually giving us new shapes, better colours and more floriferous plants. The incorporation into breeding programmes of miniature plants (some previously overlooked as being little more than weeds in their natural habitats) has given us the *mini-catts*. These small orchids with bright flowers have taught us that big is not always beautiful.

THE PLANT

The *Cattleya* alliance is found in the wild only on the American Continent, apart from some in the West Indies. Most are inhabitants of mountainous areas in the tropics and subtropics, growing as epiphytes or lithophytes. The plants are sympodial, with a creeping rhizome which is usually short, making a compact plant. New shoots arise from dormant buds at the base of the previous growth. As they develop, the stem thickens into a pseudobulb which is topped by one or more leaves which are typically thick and leathery. The leaves remain on the plant for several years, leaving a leafless backbulb which may persist for several more years before dying . The flowers arise from a terminal bud at the tip of the newest pseudobulbs and the buds may be protected by a modified leaf called a *sheath*. The flowers come in all colours except blue (some are near blue) and can last up to two months on the plant. Some flower once a year only in a particular season. Other kinds can flower two or even three times a year. Even a small collection can have something in flower at any time of the year.

HOUSING

Cattleyas can often be grown as garden plants in the tropics and subtropics by establishing them on suitable host trees or by growing them in a shadehouse. In areas subjected to long periods (several weeks) of continuous rain, they will need overhead protection to permit cyclic drying out of the roots. Further from the equator some cool growing species can still be grown outside in this manner. However, even in frost-free areas most need the closed environment of a greenhouse. Indoors, cattleyas are suitable windowsill subjects provided they can be given filtered sunlight for most of the day.

TEMPERATURE

Minimum night temperatures of 10°C (50°F) to 15°C (60°F) are the ideal. However, many adult cattleyas not in flower or active growth will tolerate minimum temperatures down to 5°C (40°F) on occasions during the coldest winter months if the air is kept dry. *Sophronitis coccinea* and its hybrids are in this category. On the other hand, many of the large flowered yellow cattleyas will sulk if kept too cold for too long. All cattleyas resent strong draughts of very cold air. Daytime air temperatures should ideally seldom exceed 30°C (86°F), but the plants will tolerate short periods up to 38°C (100°F) if leaf temperatures can be kept down, humidity is not too low and there is a temperature drop at night. Remember that all these temperatures are measured in the shade.

LIGHT

In a shadehouse 50 per cent of full sunlight is the normal maximum. In a greenhouse they will grow and flower well with a light intensity of 2000 foot-candles. In cold winter months it will be possible to give somewhat more, but in hot weather restrict the light by shading to whatever extent is necessary to keep the leaves cool to the touch. If the leaves are warm, this is just tolerable. If they are hot to the touch the plants will be under great stress. Leaves of an olive-green colour are getting all the light they need. Deep green leaves indicate too little, and yellow leaves too much light intensity respectively.

WATERING

Allow the roots and growing medium to dry out between waterings. If the plants are due to be watered and the weather is sunless and cold, do not water. They will come to no harm if kept dry for an extended period under these conditions, particularly if not in active growth. Frequent watering is usually necessary in hot, bright, summer weather, but be careful with plants in very large pots which can be dry on the top and and wet in the middle. Nutrients are best included in the water with nitrogen at 100 ppm. If using slow-release fertilisers, keep them on top of the growing medium.

POTTING

Do not pot on to a larger pot until absolutely necessary, that is, until leading growths have grown over the rim of the pot or are about to. Follow the procedures and aftercare outlined in Chapter Seven. Do not over-pot. Choose the smaller size container if in doubt, one that will just accommodate two years' growth. Use the growing medium favoured by successful growers in your area or try the mix for cattleyas as described in Chapter Six. Ensure that the rhizome of the leading growth (or growths) rests on the top of (not under) the growing medium even if this means that the back or older side of the plant is too low or up in the air. The best time to repot is when new roots have just appeared from the base of a leading growth. Cattleyas are difficult to maintain in a healthy state in very large pots. There comes a time when it is better to divide a plant into several pieces rather than move it to a yet larger container. This is discussed next.

PROPAGATION

Cattleyas can be readily grown from seed and they can be tissue-cultured to produce mericlones. Mature plants can be divided into two or more pieces by severing through the rhizome. In a straightforward case of a plant of, say, eight bulbs with only one leading growth, the cut should be made to leave two divisions of four bulbs each. The back division will be incapable of making any new roots but one of the dormant buds may be coaxed into life if it is kept in a warm humid shady place. A plant can be divided into as many pieces as there are leading growths with one or more back divisions left over. Try and have not less than four bulbs per division. They should be firmly staked if at all insecure. If the rhizome is cut a few months before repotting the otherwise dormant back division will be encouraged to break into growth before being disturbed. When eventually potted on its own, it will then get established more quickly.

PESTS AND DISEASES

Some *Cattleya* problems to watch out for are:

Insects The mature leaves are too tough and unpalatable for insects, but tender new growths and flowers can be attacked by mealybug, aphids and scale, among others. The tiny, root-nibbling snail which dwells in the pot likes cattleyas.

Leaf and bulb rots Use surgery and the treatment suggested in Chapter Eight. A quick-spreading rot can start at the junction of the flower stem and pseudobulb shortly after flowering. Prevent infection by stripping away all dead sheaths and cutting the flower stem very short.

Sheath rots Strip away pseudobulb sheaths if they show any sign of decay. Flower sheaths should be removed immediately they show any sign of turning yellow — better that the young flower buds remain unprotected rather than succumb to infection from a decaying sheath.

Shrivelled pseudobulbs These may indicate disease or lack of water due to stress (perhaps following repotting), too infrequent watering, or loss of the root system due to too frequent watering.

SOME SPECIES

Sadly, *Cattleya labiata*, the very first *Cattleya* brought into cultivation, is not common in collections today. This and its closely related species and varieties have been largely abandoned by growers in favour of the magnificent modern hybrids developed from them. The *Cattleya* alliance does however include a large number of popular species grown for an intrinsic and distinctive appeal which is often lost in their hybrids if they have any. A representative selection of these is listed below:

Brassavola (=Rhyncholaelia) glauca A small growing plant from Central America. The leaves have a bluish-grey bloom. It bears solitary, heavy textured, long lasting pale-green flowers about 11 cm across. This species likes to be dried out quickly after being watered.

Broughtonia sanguinea This small plant from the West Indies bears round, 2 cm or larger, rose-coloured flowers which open in succession on long stems. Some near-red cultivars have appeared. There are also white and yellow forms which are less vigorous. There are conflicting opinions as to the best way to grow these plants but the more vigorous of nursery-raised seedlings are not too fussy. The plant grows well on a slab. It can be flowered at any time of the year.

Cattleya aurantiaca A medium-sized plant from Central America. It bears clusters of bright orange flowers 4 cm or larger across. In some inferior cultivars the flowers do not open fully. Summer to autumn flowering. *C. aurantiaca* is in the ancestry of many highly coloured hybrids.

Cattleya walkeriana (The modern spelling is supposed to be 'walkerana'.) A small plant from Brazil with relatively large 10 cm flowers. Differs from most cattleyas in that the flowers are produced on a stem which arises from the base of the pseudobulb. There are many colour forms, including pure white. Flowers from autumn to spring. The plant likes to be kept on the dry side when not in active growth.

Encyclia citrina (syn.*Cattleya citrina*) A medium-sized, high-altitude, cool growing plant from Mexico. It has greyish-green leaves and waxy, fragrant, glistening citron-yellow flowers which do not fully open. The plant and inflorescence tend to be pendulous and the pot or basket in which it is grown may have to be tilted to allow for this. Flowers in the spring, occasionally at other times. The plant should be kept on the dry side when not in active growth.

Encyclia mariae (syn. *Epidendrum mariae*) Another cool growing plant similar to the one just described, except that it grows upright and the flowers are quite different. The 6 cm-wide flowers have glossy, jade-green petals and sepals and a large white lip. Flowers in summer.

Epidendrum radicans (= *Epidendrum ibaguense*) This reed-stemmed *Epidendrum* does not have pseudobulbs similar to other members of the *Cattleya* alliance listed here. Instead, it has a canelike stem up to a metre high bearing many leaves and aerial roots and topped by many 3 cm flowers which open in succession. The flower colour is variable but typically orange-red. The column and the lip form a cross, hence the common name of 'crucifix orchid'. This terrestrial or semi-terrestrial orchid is a tall subject for a small greenhouse but can be established in a garden even in temperate climates if given a sunny, frost-free location where it can be almost always in bloom.

Laelia anceps A popular cool growing species from Mexico with a high light requirement. Temperatures down to almost freezing point can be tolerated and it can be grown in a shadehouse in areas not subject to heavy frosts. Two to five star-shaped 10 cm flowers are borne on long, jointed stems. Flower colour is typically purple but there are white and white with coloured lip forms. Flowers in autumn.

Sophronitis coccinea (syn. *Sophronitis grandiflora*) The leaves and pseudobulbs resemble a miniature *Cattleya* but an adult flowering plant can be accommodated in a 5 cm pot. Good forms of the species have full, flat, scarlet flowers 6 cm or more across which often seem ridiculously large in relation to the size of the plant. Few growers can resist the opportunity to acquire these plants but unfortunately they are not always easy subjects and there is conflicting advice as to their correct culture. They will tolerate low nighttime temperatures, down to 5°C (42°F), for periods in the winter. They sulk if subjected to too much heat in a greenhouse in summer. They can be grown on slabs. Flowers appear from winter through to spring, from half-matured new growths. There are some very similar species known under various names, including *Sophronitis mantiqueirae, Sophronitis wittigiana, Sophronitis brevipedunculata* and a diminutive distinct *Sophronitis cernua*. *Sophronitis* species have been much used in the breeding of the so called mini-catts and are in the background of many red hybrids in the *Cattleya* alliance.

Cymbidium

Chapter Eleven

CYMBIDIUMS

HISTORY

Modern cymbidiums are grown in great quantities both by commercial growers for cut flowers and by hobbyists for their floral beauty. The spikes of heavy textured flowers are long lasting (up to two months on the plant and up to half that time when cut), and pack and travel well, hence their suitability for the cut-flower trade. The flowers have a serene and compelling beauty. Just their scent (if it can be called that) will raise the pulse of an enthusiast on entering a greenhouse or orchid show where top quality hybrids are displayed. Yet it was not always so. Although some of the cooler growing species from the Himalayan foothills were grown in English conservatories in Victorian times, any popularity they enjoyed was probably due in a large measure to the graceful foliage and ease of culture. The flowers then were just flowers to the horticulturist, hardly a threat to the flamboyant cattleyas.

Although cymbidiums were first grown in Europe in the middle of the last century, they have been cultivated in the Orient since at least the time of Confucius some 2500 years ago. There, beauty was often seen to be in the graceful foliage rather than in the flowers. In Europe the *Cymbidium* suddenly emerged as a plant of horticultural merit with the introduction into breeding programmes of some chance tetraploids just after World War I. Although many of our modern hybrid cymbidiums are diploids (and very useful breeding plants), most of the top-quality cultivars are tetraploids or triploids. These tend to have larger and heavier flowers with broader sepals, petals and lips. Often, too, they have shorter spikes with fewer flowers and can be slower growers.

There are no blue cymbidiums and the reds are not yet quite as bright as we would like them to be. However, the other colours are all now available in modern hybrids and in a range of plant sizes. It is just possible to have cymbidiums in flower in each month of the year in a large collection, but they bloom in greatest numbers from mid-winter to late spring. Development of the modern hybrid was initiated in England but they are now popular in many countries, including USA (particularly California), Australia, New Zealand, Japan and South Africa. Standard cymbidiums are difficult to flower in the tropics. Here attempts at cultivation are likely to be limited to tropical species, usually miniatures, or hybrids based on them.

THE PLANT

There are about 50 cymbidium species, limited to an area extending from the Himalayan foothills to southern Japan and Taiwan and southwards through South-East Asia down as far as Australia. They are variously terrestrial, lithophytic or epiphytic in habit. They are sympodial, successive growths being joined by a rhizome, although this is very short, making for a compact plant. The pseudobulbs are somewhat compressed and the leaves are usually long and strap like. The leaves should persist for several years before dying and dropping off, leaving a leafless but still alive, pseudobulb, then referred to as a backbulb.

THE FLOWER SPIKE

The flower spike usually develops from a node at the base of the pseudobulb. With an immature growth where the pseudobulb is not fully formed, the spike may appear to emerge from the axil of one of the outside leaves. Although the flower spike appears early in the season, the initial development is slow, often not appearing to grow at all for a month or two but then elongating rapidly as the flowering season approaches. When they first appear it is often difficult to distinguish flower spikes from new vegetative shoots. Spikes at this stage tend to be round, bullet shaped, smaller in diameter at the base, grow out at an angle and are often pigmented. New vegetative growths in contrast are flat, wider at the base, curve upwards and are seldom heavily pigmented.

The spike on a modern hybrid usually bears between six and 16 flowers, sometimes more or less. They frequently need to be staked to prevent them falling over or to force them to grow upright if the grower wants them that way. In the latter case they must be staked and trained and secured with ties up the length of the spike while it is still developing. A naturally pendulous spike will only elongate if left that way. Do not stake such a spike in an erect position as it will remain stunted. A merely arching spike can be staked upright but will often look better if supported in its natural position.

TERMS USED

Cymbidiums are grouped, for horticultural purposes, into a few different categories, with no universal agreement about exactly where the boundaries between the groups are. The terms most commonly used are:

Miniatures These are smaller, compact plants due to the influence of a small growing species in the ancestry.

Novelties Some orchid societies place a restriction, for judging purposes, on the size of the flowers of plants qualifying for the miniature category. If the flowers are too large, yet show the influence of a miniature ancestor, they can be called *novelties* or sometimes *intermediate cymbidiums*.

Polymins These were the progeny of a miniature species and a tetraploid standard. However, as polyploidy is now common in all categories, the term is falling into disuse.

Standard cymbidiums Almost anything other than miniatures or novelties. These are larger plants with larger flowers.

Pure colours Largely developed in Australia, these hybrids have no purple pigment and the only colours in the flowers are white and peculiar shades of yellow and green. Sometimes called *albinos* or *concolours*.

HOUSING

Cymbidiums are generally considered to be cool growing orchids, tolerating quite low temperatures but not liking excessive heat in the summer. They can be grown in the garden, preferably in containers, in a situation where they receive filtered sunlight throughout most of the day. A tree which allows 50 per cent of the sunlight to reach the plant is suitable. In frost-free areas they can be left outside all year and make suitable shadehouse subjects under 50 per cent shadecloth. However the quality of blooms will be higher if the plants are sheltered from rain from the onset of winter until flowering has been completed. In any event, a plant with flower spikes will need protection from frost. Many growers with only a few plants and no greenhouse manage them by having a suitable patio, sunporch or window in which to flower the plants, leaving them outside during the summer. Cymbidiums often produce the finest flowers if grown in a closed greenhouse the year round.

TEMPERATURE AND LIGHT

Cymbidiums which are grown and hardened outside will tolerate more light and lower temperatures than those in a closed greenhouse. In fact the plants grown outside seem to require higher light levels to initiate flowering. Almost 4000 foot-candles is correct for plants grown in a shadehouse. In a greenhouse up to 3000 foot-candles is normal, but it may have to be reduced in summer to keep temperatures down. Flowers need to be kept cool and flowering plants in a greenhouse will in any event need to have the light reduced to 1500 foot-candles or, without fan-assisted ventilation, less than this.

Cymbidiums will tolerate temperatures down to freezing point. Plants grown outside will survive several degrees of frost without suffering too much damage provided there are no flower spikes. In general, greenhouse temperatures should only occasionally go below 5°C (40°F) during winter nights. A minimum nearer 10°C (50°F) is a better figure to aim at for most nights to ensure good quality flowers, especially with some of the miniature hybrids. Cool night temperatures are said to be one of the factors necessary to initiate flowers, and to be the reason why standard cymbidiums are difficult to flower in the tropics. High day temperatures are not usually a problem in the garden or shadehouse unless the plants are exposed to hot, dry winds. In a greenhouse temperatures should ideally not exceed 32°C (90°F) regularly in summer. They will survive higher temperatures if shaded heavily, but try to maintain humidity in these conditions.

WATERING

Most cymbidiums are treated as semi-terrestrials in cultivation. In cold winter weather allow the growing medium to almost but not quite dry out between waterings. In summer do not allow it to approach dryness — keep the growing medium moist but not waterlogged. The plants will suffer no permanent damage if dried out to the point where the pseudobulbs shrivel, as may happen during your summer vacation if nobody waters them in your absence. However, they will be visibly checked and the quality of the following season's flowers may suffer.

GROWING MEDIA AND NUTRITION

Literally hundreds of cymbidium media recipes have been published and it has been said that these orchids have been observed growing, after a fashion, in almost anything, including garden soil. Pine bark is popular, or the reader may wish to try the mix for cymbidiums in Chapter Six. Cymbidiums are heavy feeders and will respond to nutrients (use a 150 to 170 ppm nitrogen formula) in the water supply. Alternatively, slow-release fertilisers work well with cymbidiums. They can be incorporated throughout the medium at the outset, but when exhausted, further applications can only be applied to the surface.

POTTING

Plastic containers, even plastic bags, are most commonly used, although some growers prefer clay pots. Cymbidiums can be grown in a slightly larger pot than would be selected for, say, cattleyas, but do not over-pot. When moving a plant to a larger pot it is best to remove all the old growing medium. Repotting is best done in the spring with the object of getting the plants established before put under stress by summer heat. Cymbidiums can be potted on indefinitely but there comes a time when the next size container is just too large to manage. When this happens, or when the plant develops a lot of backbulbs, it must be broken into pieces.

PROPAGATION

A plant can be broken or divided up into single bulbs by cutting through the rhizomes. Even the old bulbs and leafless backbulbs which would otherwise remain dormant will be encouraged to make new shoots just by the act of removing them. Divisions of one new shoot with one or two green bulbs behind them make better plants in the long run than larger or smaller divisions. A root-bound plant may be impossible to disentangle unless the bottom half of the root ball is first cut off with a sterile knife. This apparently brutal treatment usually leaves the divisions with more attached roots at the end of the process. Under-pot the divisions to assist their initial establishment. Backbulbs without live roots are best planted singly rather deeply in sand or sphagnum moss and potted up normally after they have made a new shoot.

The plants are best broken up as early in the season as possible, the flower spikes being removed as soon as practicable to this end. Even so, the shock may prevent the division from flowering the following season. Plants broken up in late summer after flowers have been initiated will flower, but flower quality will be poor and the divisions will be slow to establish. Cymbidiums are readily propagated both from seed and by tissue culture.

PESTS AND DISEASES

Some more commonly encountered *Cymbidium* pests and diseases are:

Insects and mites Two-spotted mite will almost certainly get into a collection at some time. Be watchful and spray before large populations build up. Scale insects and aphids are occasionally a problem.

Flower spotting Caused by very high humidity combined with low temperatures. Some cultivars are more susceptible. A gentle movement of warmer air over the flowers during cold nights or at other times when the risk is present will prevent this trouble.

Leaf tip dieback There is disagreement over the precise cause, but plants watered with rainwater seem immune. Not serious if not too extreme.

Red lips If followed by premature collapse of the flower, indicates it has been pollinated or pollinia removed.

Brown lips Frequent low temperatures almost down to freezing accompanied by high humidities can cause flowers to open with necrotic brown lip margins.

Yellow buds Followed by bud drop, these may be due to exposure to sudden temperature rises or bright sunlight. Some cultivars are more prone to it than others.

Shrivelled bulbs In summer this problem can be due to a combination of leaving the growing medium too dry for too long, lower humidities and high light intensities. In winter it usually indicates decay of the root system.

Failure to flower If a healthy mature plant regularly fails to flower, try giving it more light. Some cultivars are genetically shy flowerers, i.e., it is an inherited defect. Leaving a year's flower spikes on too long can result in no flowers the next season.

SPECIES

Unfortunately most of the species used to create the modern hybrids are seldom found in collections today. Some still cultivated for their intrinsic appeal include:

Cymbidium tracyanum A popular epiphyte from Burma and Thailand with up to 20 large reddish flowers. Flowers early in the season. Flowers are scented but do not keep well. Easy to cultivate.

Cymbidium lowianum A large semi-terrestrial species found from northern India to China. Long arching flower spikes with 30 or more yellow-green flowers with characteristic red, v-shaped band on lip. Easy to cultivate.

Cymbidium devonianum A popular smallish species from northern India. It has wide leaves and does not look like a *Cymbidium* out of flower. The pendulous spike of many dark-brownish flowers with pink lips hangs down and must be trained over the side of the pot.

Cymbidium canaliculatum A distinctive species from Australia with thick leaves. Popular is var. *sparksii* which has up to 50 dark red, almost black, 20 mm flowers and has a reputation for being difficult to cultivate, but is worth the effort. It should be treated as an epiphyte, given more light than most cymbidiums, not allowed to get too cold and allowed to dry out completely between waterings.

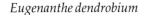
Eugenanthe dendrobium

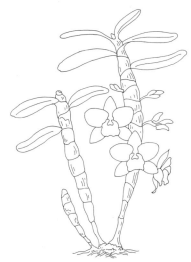

Chapter Twelve

DENDROBIUMS

THE GENUS

With about 1400 species this is numerically perhaps the largest genus in the orchid family. The plants are epiphytes or lithophytes and the growth habit is sympodial. The geographical range is the same as for cymbidiums but extends further east to islands in the South Pacific and south as far as New Zealand. There is such diversity in the species that it is difficult to choose a typical plant to describe. Some have pseudobulbs but in most of those cultivated the stem is thickened into what is better described as a cane. The natural habitat in, say, the tropics, can vary from hot lowland forests to elevations of over 3000 m in New Guinea. The requirements of dendrobiums in cultivation are accordingly also diverse.

The salient feature of the flower in *Dendrobium* is the spur formed by the lateral sepals and an extended column foot. Taxonomically, the genus has been classified (with some uncertainty) into a number of sections. It is convenient to discuss the plants and their cultivation under these sections. It is not possible to mention them all. The vast majority of the dendrobiums seen in cultivation are, however, in the few sections listed below. Unless otherwise mentioned, all should be grown in coarse bark or a mix suitable for cattleyas and allowed to dry out between waterings. If uncertain about the requirements of a species, treat it as you would a *Cattleya* but give a little more light and keep fairly dry in the winter, particularly if there is any tendency to drop leaves at that time. Some species do not like pots and prefer to be mounted on a slab. Watch out for mealybug in the new growths. Two-spotted mite occasionally gets established on kinds with thin leaves.

SECTION *CALLISTA*

This small section contains some plants which produce spectacular floral displays, mainly in the spring. The deep green leaves are confined to the upper portion of the swollen pseudobulb and the often pendulous flower spike, bearing clusters of up to 15 flowers, comes from one of the upper nodes. Light, temperature and nutrients as suggested for cattleyas will suit them. However, do not supply any nutrients after late summer. Water less frequently and give them more light in winter.

Dendrobium aggregatum A dwarfish species with clustered 8-cm-high pseudobulbs topped by a single leaf. The fragrant 5 cm flowers hang in clusters and deepen with age to a golden yellow.

Dendrobium chrysotoxum The stout canes are some 20 cm tall. The clusters of 5 cm waxy golden flowers often come from older canes.

Dendrobium densiflorum The plant has club-shaped four-angled pseudobulbs or canes some 30 cm tall. The 5 cm yellow flowers with orange lips make a spectacular sight but are not particularly long lasting. A slightly cooler growing species.

Dendrobium farmeri Similar plant to the above with its four-angled pseudobulbs. The spikes of densely packed apple-blossom-pink or white 5 cm flowers last up to two weeks.

Other species cultivated These include *D. capillipes*, *D. griffithianum*, and *D. thyrsiflorum*.

Hybrids There are some hybrids but they are not common. A few hybrids with genera in other sections have been recorded but they are even less commonly seen.

SECTION *CERATOBIUM*

There are many species in this section and some confusion in nomenclature which has only recently been clarified. Some species have been known under different names. Further, some are found over a vast geographic range (over 2000 km east to west for *Dendrobium gouldii*) and there can be considerable variation within a species. These are warm growing evergreen plants with the leaves usually confined to the upper half of the canes, which may be 50 cm high or several times that length in some species. Flower spikes bearing many flowers come from the axils of the upper leaves. The flowers are usually long lasting and come in shades of purple, white, green and yellow. The sepals and often the petals are twisted, giving the section the common name of 'antelope orchids'. There has been much hybridisation with section *Phalaenanthe* and occasionally others to produce an enormous range of important hybrids which are commonly cultivated in tropical countries by hobbyists and for the commercial cut-flower trade.

Ceratobium dendrobiums like bright light (about the same as for cymbidiums under greenhouse culture) and warmth, with a minimum night temperature of 15°C (60°F). Use the same mix as for cattleyas, but keep them in small pots. Water and supply nutrients throughout the year. Some of the species cultivated are *D. affine* (with white flowers which resemble those in section *Phalaenanthe*), *D. antennatum, D. canaliculatum* (a smaller plant than the others), *D. gouldii, D. taurinum, D. tangerinum* (often called *D. strebloceras*) and *D. undulatum*.

SECTION *DENDROCORYNE*

Although the name may be formidable, this popular section includes some well known natives of Australia. The plants grow as epiphytes or lithophytes along the eastern ranges. A single species may inhabit an enormous range of latitudes (3000 km north to south for *Dendrobium speciosum*) and can vary in tolerance to cold. In cultivation most are treated as cool growing orchids and will grow in a shadehouse under 50 per cent shadecloth, tolerating temperatures almost down to freezing. They should be kept on the dry side during the winter and prefer to be brought under cover then and until flowering has finished in the spring. In a greenhouse give the plants the same light as cymbidiums. Potting media and nutrition are the same as as for cattleyas. A brief description of some of the plants cultivated follows, but bear in mind that even within a species there is wide variation in flower colour and plant form, including the length of the canes. Leaves are confined to the upper half of the canes and flower spikes come from the upper leaf axils.

Dendrobium falcorostrum The canes are typically about 20 cm high and bear many 4 cm or larger white, fragrant flowers. A cool growing species which resents root disturbance and is often grown on a slab.

Dendrobium kingianum A widely and easily grown species which often succeeds in the hands of someone who knows nothing about orchids. The canes are swollen at the base and may vary from 5 cm to over 40 cm in length, but are commonly 20 cm. The 2.5 cm flowers vary in colour from white through pink to purple. Aerial plantlets develop and can be potted up or left on the plant where they will produce flowers the following season.

Dendrobium speciosum   The largest plant in this section, sometimes up to 50 cm high, with stout pseudobulbs and leathery leaves. The flowers spikes are densely packed with many 5 cm cream to yellow flowers. A fairly hardy species, some varieties withstanding light frosts.

Dendrobium delicatum   Said to be a natural hybrid between *D. kingianum* and *D. speciosum* but has also been hybridised artificially. Widely grown.

Hybrids   Enterprising hybridists, mainly in Australia, are producing many hybrids within this section and with some other sections. Some of these show promise of being easy to grow plants of horticultural merit.

Other species   Also cultivated are *D. adae, D. fleckeri, D. gracilicaule* and *D. tetragonum.*

SECTION *EUGENANTHE*

These are referred to in some literature as 'soft cane' dendrobiums. The species in this section are more often than not found in areas with warm wet summers and cool dry winters. Many are deciduous, dropping the leaves from mature canes in the winter. The plants which are cultivated in the greatest numbers are hybrids derived mainly from *Dendrobium nobile.*

Dendrobium nobile   A widespread spring-flowering species growing from the Himalayas across through South China down as far as Vietnam. It grows at elevations up to 1500 m. The plant is found in varying forms but typically has finger-thick canes up to 50 cm high. Flowers up to 8 cm wide, in shades of white and lavender, come from nodes on mature canes which often drop their leaves and have a yellowish appearance.

In cultivation, the plants will grow in coarse bark or the mix as for cattleyas. During the summer months give the same light intensity as for cattleyas and do not let the plants quite dry out between waterings. Provide nutrients with an approximate 100 ppm nitrogen formula. Do not use any slow-release fertilisers and cease supplying nutrients from late or even mid summer until flower buds are well developed. In winter give more light, dry out between waterings and leave the medium dry while weather is very cold — even to the point of allowing the canes to shrivel slightly. While dry they will tolerate temperatures down to 3 °C (37 °F). Adventitious growths may develop from nodes instead of flowers. This is not always desirable and is encouraged by applying nutrients too late in the season. When the growths develop roots they can be potted up to make new plants.

Dendrobium nobile hybrids Hybridisation has given us tetraploid plants with thicker shorter canes and heavier, larger, better shaped, long lasting flowers with a colour range from pure white through yellow, pink and dark purple. Modern superior hybrids are often called *Yamamoto hybrids* after the Japanese breeder who took a major role in developing them. They flower more reliably than the species, but culture is the same. The flowers last longer and in better condition if kept cool and shaded.

Other species Some with the same cultural requirements as *Dendrobium nobile* are *D. friedericksianum*, *D. heterocarpum* (syn. *D. aureum*), *D. wardianum* and *D. loddigesii*. The last mentioned is a charming prostrate miniature.

SECTION *NIGROHIRSUTAE*

Some of these Asian species have black or brownish hairs, particularly on the leaf sheaths. Canes tend to be cylindrical with deep green leaves down much of their length. The flowers are white and although somewhat papery, are long lasting. The same potting media, nutrition and light intensities recommended for cattleyas will suit these plants. Some tropical species prefer minimum night temperatures of 12 °C to 15 °C (55 °F to 60 °F) but others from higher higher elevations can be grown in cooler environments. A few hybrids are available, some very beautiful, but the following species are found in collections. Flowering season is variable, with the cooler growers tending towards spring.

Dendrobium cruentum Greenish 6 cm flowers with a bright orange throat borne on 30 cm canes. Warm growing.

Dendrobium dearei Canes 30 cm to 60 cm in height. Pure white 6 cm or larger flowers with a green throat. Warm growing.

Dendrobium formosum Canes 30 cm or longer. Large (up to 12 cm) white flowers with a yellow-orange throat. Warm growing.

Dendrobium infundibilum (**syn. *Dendrobium jamesianum***) Somewhat similar to *D. formosum*, but flowers are smaller. A cool growing plant.

Dendrobium sanderae Resembles *D. dearei* but with taller stems and larger flowers which have purple to bright red side lobes on the lip. Warm growing.

Dendrobium schutzei Similar to *D. dearei* but shorter canes and larger flowers. A fine warm growing species.

Dendrobium bellatulum A dwarf species with canes under 8 cm high and relatively large white flowers. Cooler growing.

SECTION *PHALAENANTHE*

The plants in this very important section have cylindrical canes slightly swollen in the middle with a few rather leathery leaves near the top. The flower spikes bear up to a dozen (or more in well grown specimens) long lasting flowers. Flowering season is variable, mainly autumn. As a general guide, give the plants the same light, growing media and nutrition as for cattleyas, but a minimum night temperature of 15°C (60°F) for best results. Do not over-pot them. The species come from areas with hot, wet summers and drier winters. The plants like high humidity when in active growth but should be dried out (and quickly) between waterings and allowed to remain dry for a period in winter before watering again. They can be grown, after a fashion, with minimum temperatures of 10°C (50°F) if kept very dry during the winter (the leaves may fall off under these conditions), but this takes some skill. These are tropical plants.

There are only a few species in this section. The two best known are *Dendrobium phalaenopsis* (not to be confused with the genus *Phalaenopsis*) and *Dendrobium bigibbum*. Both are variable and some authorities suspect they are merely forms of the same species, which grows naturally from northern Queensland to New Guinea. *Dendrobium bigibbum*, the Cooktown orchid, is the state floral emblem of Queensland. The plants found in cultivation labelled *D. phalaenopsis* are likely to be the product of line breeding over several generations. These modern tetraploid strains have large (typically about 8 cm) long lasting (over two months) round flowers. They vary in colour from white through pink to the deepest of red-purples. Together with the hybrids with other sections (particularly section *Ceretobium*), they are part of a multi-million-dollar cut-flower orchid business in Hawaii and some Asian countries.

OTHER DENDROBIUMS

There are many other species worth cultivating. A few are:

Dendrobium arachnites A dwarfish species with unusual bright orange, upside-down flowers. Flowers in spring and seems to like being grown the same way as *D. nobile*. A species with similar flowers is *D. unicum*.

Dendrobium lawsii A cool growing species from New Guinea. Bright orange to red flowers are borne on thin canes up to 25 cm long and inclined to be pendulous.

Dendrobium sophronites A miniature orchid from high altitudes (up to 3000 m and higher) in New Guinea. A 5 cm pot can hold a plant with 20 pseudobulbs. The flowers are literally larger than the pseudobulbs and leaves, last for at least three months and come in a potpourri of colours ranging from yellow through orange, red and mauve. Perhaps best grown on a slab, the plant will tolerate cold nights but not hot greenhouses and should not be left dry at the roots for any length of time. *D. cuthbertsonii* is a similar, or perhaps the same, species.

Dendrobium trigonopus A compact plant with 15 cm canes covered in black hairs. The waxy 5 cm flowers are yellow with a glistening texture. Flowers in spring. Cultivation as for cattleyas seems to suit it.

Dendrobium victoriae-reginae Blue or violet flowers about 3 cm across are borne on long, thin, branching canes. Always attracts attention when exhibited. Cultivate as for cattleyas but it is generally regarded as a cool growing orchid.

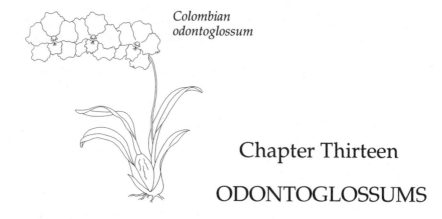

Colombian odontoglossum

Chapter Thirteen

ODONTOGLOSSUMS

THE ALLIANCE

The *Odontoglossum* genus is a member of a subtribe in which are grouped nearly 60 other genera, all confined to the American continent and the Caribbean area. Orchid growers refer to many of them as the *Odontoglossum alliance* or (more correctly, botanically) to all of them as the *Oncidium alliance*. This chapter covers only the *Odontoglossum* genus itself and some of the intergeneric hybrids made with it. Some of the other genera in the alliance and their hybrids are referred to in Chapter Fourteen. They are all sympodial in growth and mainly epiphytes. The flower spikes arise from the base of the new growth or mature pseudobulb. Potting procedures, growing media and nutrition as for cattleyas are usually suitable. The other environmental factors can vary according to the species. Be on guard against the tiny root-nibbling snail which has a particular liking for some of these plants. Leafless pseudobulbs which turn brown and commence to decay should be immediately removed by severing not the rhizome but the bulb at the base and then applying a fungicide.

COLOMBIAN ODONTOGLOSSUMS

These are species which grow in the high Andes virtually on the equator but at elevations of 2000 m or even 3000 m. The most famous is *Odontoglossum crispum*. Well grown plants have 7 cm high green pseudobulbs, leaves 30 cm or longer, and flower spikes bearing up to 20 or so flowers up to 10 cm across. Most of the plants labelled *Odontoglossum crispum* now in cultivation are pure white forms and the result of over 80 years of line breeding. The original plants (seldom seen today) were often blotched with chocolate, purple and reddish markings, and these colours come through in modern hybrids. *Cochlioda noezliana*, a cool growing species from Peru with small scarlet flowers, has been crossed with *Odontoglossum* to give the intergeneric hybrid *Odontioda*. Some solid red odontiodas inherit their colour from this species.

Colombian odontoglossums and the odontiodas bred from them are among the most beautiful flowers in the orchid family. Unfortunately if you live at sea level in the tropics or anywhere with long, very hot dry summers you will only be able to envy those who have the cooler climate which permits their culture. The further one is from the equator (unless at a high elevation), the easier they are to grow. Optimum daytime temperature is about 20°C (68°F). The plants will cease to grow as temperatures approach 30°C (86°F) and will go into a decline if daily maximums exceed that figure, more quickly if the relative humidity is low. They respond, sometimes sensationally well, to evaporative cooling systems. Try and keep them cool in hot weather by regular misting. In summer put them near the floor of the greenhouse where it is cooler and ensure there is plenty of air movement, or transfer them to a shadehouse.

In frost-free areas good plants have been cultivated where they are left permanently in a sheltered shadehouse with overhead rain protection. Colombian odontoglossums and odontiodas will tolerate temperatures almost down to freezing or even being left outside and subjected to weeks of cold rain. However, they will not thrive under these conditions. A nightly minimum of 10°C (45°F) is usually recommended, but they will respond to slightly higher minimums. In short, the plants like a fairly even temperature, not too hot and not too cold.

If you can provide the optimum temperatures, the plants are easy to grow. The other aspects to consider are:

Watering Do not allow the growing medium to remain dry in the summer. In winter the plants are best dried out well between waterings but will appreciate overhead misting while dry at the roots.

Light In a greenhouse, less than for cattleyas. About 1500 foot-candles is the maximum. In a shadehouse in summer admit not more than 30 per cent to 40 per cent of natural sunlight. Bronze colours appearing in the foliage indicate that the light intensity is at the upper limit.

Flowering There is no particular season. Plants seem to flower eight to ten months after the last flower spike was removed. Do not leave flower spikes on the plant after the leading bulb starts to shrivel. Flowers which appear in the summer do not have the quality of those which open in winter and spring.

Propagation   Only divide large plants. Difficult to propagate from leafless backbulbs. Not easy to tissue culture. Seedlings from good parents are available and yield a high percentage of good quality flowers. They can flower in two years from the flask. However, spikes should be removed from immature plants, otherwise they can take some years to reach the maturity necessary for quality flower production.

CENTRAL AMERICAN ODONTOGLOSSUMS

There are a number of species not very closely related to *Odontoglossum crispum* which grow at lower elevations in Central America. In general these are all marginally more tolerant of high temperatures than *O. crispum*, will take a little more light and many people find them easier to manage. A little hybridisation has been done with some, but the species below are worth growing for their intrinsic appeal. They all grow naturally in Mexico (some extend further afield) and are mostly winter to spring flowering.

Odontoglossum bictoniense   Tall, erect spikes carrying many 6 cm brown and green flowers with a heart-shaped white or pink lip. A warmer grower which has been used with Colombian odontoglossums to make distinctive hybrids.

Odontoglossum cervantesii   A small plant with three to five whitish 6 cm flowers characterised by concentric rings of reddish-brown lines which appear to be neatly drawn over the bases of the petals and sepals.

Odontoglossum grande (= Rossioglossum grande)   A medium-sized plant with spectacular large (up to 15 cm) glossy flowers which are basically yellow but heavily shaded and barred with chestnut brown.

Odontoglossum pendulum (syn. *Odontoglossum citrosmum*)   A charming species, always admired when in flower. It has glossy green pseudobulbs and leathery dark green leaves. The pendulous flower spike emerges from an immature new growth and bears many 6 cm white flowers flushed with pink. The plant may not flower unless it is kept dry during the winter months (to the point where the pseudobulbs shrivel) and preferably given more light at this time.

Odontoglossum pulchellum (= Osmoglossum pulchellum)   A smallish, popular plant with erect spikes of up to 8 waxy, glistening-white 3 cm flowers with a bright yellow disc on the lip. The flowers are upside down with the lip uppermost. Very fragrant.

Odontoglossum rossii   A similar plant to *O. cervantesii*. Flowers are larger and variable in colour, the base of the sepals usually being blotched with reddish-brown but without the concentric rings.

Odontoglossum uro-skinneri Somewhat resembles *O. bictoniense* but has larger flowers. Possibly requires a little more shade.

INTERGENERIC HYBRIDS

A bewildering number of hybrids have been made between the various genera in the alliance. An equally perplexing array of intergeneric names have had to be created to label them and few growers attempt to remember them all. Much effort has recently gone into crossing *Odontoglossum crispum* type hybrids with other warmer growing genera with the idea of introducing heat tolerance into the former. Some of the individual qualities of *O. crispum* usually have to be traded off to achieve this goal. Nevertheless some very attractive and easy-to-grow, new-look flowers are being created. The more widely grown of these intergenerics are discussed below. Many tolerate higher temperatures than *Odontoglossum crispum*.

Aspoglossum. (Odontoglossum x Aspasia) The somewhat dull coloured *Aspasia* injects warmth tolerance but in some crosses smaller flower size and flower count. Flower shape is better than might be expected.

Beallara (Brassia x Miltonia x Cochlioda x Odontoglossum) The best known is *Beallara* Tahoma Glacier (*Miltassia* Cartagena x *Odontioda* Alaskan Sunset) which is a strong plant with greenish-white flowers up to 15 cm somewhat reminiscent of a *Maclellanara*. There are others with stronger colours.

Colmanara (Miltonia x Odontoglossum x Oncidium) These are mostly warmer growers but much depends upon the particular species in the ancestry.

Maclellanara (Oncidium x Odontoglossum x Brassia) There are not many of these. The shape is dominated by the spidery *Brassia* and they do not much resemble *Odontoglossum crispum*. The first one, the well known and widely distributed *Maclellanara* Pagan Lovesong (*Odontocidium* Tiger Butter x *Brassia verrucosa*) is a strong grower with large star-shaped flowers.

Odontocidium (Odontoglossum x Oncidium) Variable according to the species used. Well known are the glossy yellow and brown flowers using *Oncidium tigrinum* as one parent and which is slightly more heat tolerant than *Odontoglossum crispum*. Crosses such as *Odontocidium* Tiger Butter (*Oncidium tigrinum* x *Odontoglossum* Golden Avalanche) have been used to sire the intergenerics *Wilsonara* and *Maclellanara*.

Odontonia (Miltonia* x *Odontoglossum) Those with Colombian miltonias (= *Miltoniopsis* — see Chapter Fourteen) in their ancestry are usually cool growing. Those made with *Miltonia warscewiczii* (including *Odontocidium* Debutante hybrids) may be warmer growing.

Vuylstekeara (Miltonia* x *Odontoglossum* x *Cochlioda) If the hybrid is based on a Colombian *Miltonia* (= *Miltoniopsis*), it is likely to be cooler growing, a well known example being the old but still widely grown *Vuylstekeara* Cambria 'Plush'. Hybrids with Brazilian *Miltonia* blood are warmer growing, usually with a greater number of smaller flowers.

Wilsonara (Cochlioda* x *Odontoglossum* x *Oncidium) Usually the progeny of *Odontioda* x *Oncidium*. Crosses using *Oncidium tigrinum* have been popular in recent years. A few crosses using warmer growing oncidiums show greater heat tolerance.

Oncidium

Chapter Fourteen

THE ONCIDIUM ALLIANCE

The 60-odd genera in the *Oncidium* subtribe are a diverse lot but the remaining important ones are best dealt with together, especially as there are so many intergeneric hybrids. Odontoglossums have already been covered in the previous chapter. This chapter is devoted to *Oncidium* (which gives its name to the alliance as a whole) and *Miltonia*, together with a few other genera of horticultural merit. All are natives of tropical and subtropical America and are mainly epiphytes.

ONCIDIUMS

It has been traditional to divide oncidiums into cool, intermediate and warm growers. However, in common with many orchids, some oncidiums are adaptable which probably explains why authorities do not always agree about the cultivation category to which a particular species belongs. There are about 400 *Oncidium* species. A few of those popular in cultivation are listed below. Except where otherwise indicated, potting media, light and nutrition similar to the requirements of cattleyas will suit them. All oncidiums should dry out between waterings.

Oncidiums do not suffer from any pests and diseases not found on other orchids. Mites may occasionally get established on some thin-leaved kinds and the root-nibbling snail can be a problem.

Oncidium crispum   A cool grower which will tolerate lower night temperatures than most. It has long rhizomes and long wandering roots. It is difficult to keep in a pot but does well on a slab mounted in a pot. The handsome flowers on branched spikes are up to 8 cm wide and a glistening chestnut colour with yellow markings. Do not confuse it with *Odontoglossum crispum*. Allied species with similar flowers on more compact plants include *Oncidium forbesii* and *Oncidium sarcodes*, the latter preferring warmer night temperatures. Autumn, winter and spring flowering.

Oncidium luridum   A large plant with a solitary, thick, rigid leaf and little in the way of a pseudobulb. The flowers are greenish-yellow, spotted red-brown and borne on a branching spike. The plant likes warmer night temperatures and higher light (as for cymbidiums), but not enough to burn the fleshy leaves or bring up too much red pigmentation in them. Do not water too often when the plants are in spike and continue to water infrequently through flowering and until a new vegetative growth appears. Commonly called the 'mule ear orchid'. Other closely related species include *Oncidium cavendishianum* and *Oncidium lanceanum*.

Oncidium macranthum (= Cyrtochilum macranthum)   With bright yellow flowers 8 cm or more wide on very long (up to 300 cm) branched climbing spikes, this is a spectacular species. A cool grower from the high Andes.

Oncidium papilio   The 'butterfly orchid' from the West Indies.. This species caused worldwide interest when introduced to England in 1823. It does not require too much imagination to see the 10 cm or larger brown and yellow flowers mimicking a large insect. The flowers open in succession on top of a long spike. The leaves are green but decoratively mottled red-brown, and the pseudobulbs are flattish and wrinkled. Not always easy to grow, this species seems to need conditions as for cattleyas, with night temperatures ideally a little higher and perhaps a little less light intensity. Do not allow them to remain dry at the roots for too long. *Oncidium kramerianum* is a similar species.

Oncidium tigrinum   Brownish, waxy 7 cm flowers with a startling contrasting bright yellow lip. It will grow well if given the same culture as cattleyas. Worth growing for its own sake, but famous as a parent of many odontocidiums and other intergeneric hybrids.

Oncidium varicosum   The sepals and petals are relatively small, the dominant feature being the 4 cm wide or larger yellow lip. Long spikes bear many flowers which move in the slightest breeze presenting a fanciful floral ballet, hence the common name of 'dancing lady orchid', although many other species cast in the same mould are also given this name. There are a number of hybrids with *Oncidium varicosum* ancestry which have similar shape but larger flowers (although less of them) and stronger colours. These hybrids are well worth growing and seem to tolerate a wide range of environments.

Equitant oncidiums These are sometimes called the *Variegata* oncidiums after one of the typical species, *Oncidium variegata*. This and other allied species from Florida and the West Indies have been used to create a swarm of hybrids which produce flowers the year round in a seemingly never-ending combination of bright colour patterns. The plants are small (first flowering in 5 cm pots), the leaves are arranged in the form of a small fan, and they have scarcely developed pseudobulbs. They require minimum night temperatures of 12°C (55°F) and good light, about the same as required by cymbidiums. A slight bronzing of the leaves indicates light is at a maximum. They must dry out within hours of watering and for this reason most growers mount them on slabs.

MILTONIOPSIS

There are two kinds of miltonias, the so-called Colombian miltonias (although they are found elsewhere) and the Brazilian miltonias. The taxonomists have moved the Colombian ones to the genus *Miltoniopsis*. As the two kinds are distinct and culture is slightly different, they are dealt with separately here. Many growers however still call them all miltonias and they are so regarded for hybrid registration purposes.

The general appearance of the flowers gives the plant the common name of 'pansy orchid'. The broad, rounded lip is a prominent feature of the flower. One to several flowers are borne on a spike in colours ranging from yellow and white through pink to deep red-purple. A central pattern, called a *mask*, is usually a contrasting colour, adding character to the flower. The plants have oval, compressed pseudobulbs and grey-green fragile looking leaves some 20 cm or more long. These orchids, widely grown last century, suffered a decline in interest for a time but are now once again very popular. The plants in collections are usually hybrids but the species on which these hybrids were founded, mainly *Miltonia vexillaria* and *Miltonia roezlii*, are occasionally seen.

Miltoniopsis are often classified as cool growing but like Colombian odontoglossums, it is extremes of temperature they resent. They can be cultivated with a minimum night temperature of 10°C (50°F), but are easier to grow if kept slightly warmer. Try and keep daytime temperatures below 26°C (80°F), but if they go above this, maintain good air circulation, high humidity and keep them heavily shaded. Light intensity should be about 1000 to 1500 foot-candles, or less with higher temperatures. Use potting media and nutrition as recommended for cattleyas and be careful not to over-pot. Do not leave *Miltoniopsis* dry at the roots, especially in summer when they should be watered before they have quite dried out. The plants have been grown successfully on windowsills, in the company of paphiopedilums and even with *Phalaenopsis*. *Miltoniopsis* flowers are best admired on the plant where they are quite long lasting. They do not keep well after being cut.

MILTONIA

Brazilian miltonias, at least the species, have more star-shaped flowers and not quite such a generous lip as their Colombian relatives. They are also more adaptable to differing environments and for this reason have a reputation of being easier to grow. Most will thrive if grown with cattleyas using the same growing media and drying out between waterings. The species most often seen in collections are the *Miltonia spectabilis* (white to deep purple), *Miltonia clowesii* and *Miltonia flavescens*, the latter two species being predominantly yellow. All are moderate-sized plants. They are summer blooming and the flowers last well when cut.

In recent years much hybridisation has been done with Brazilian miltonias and many superior, easier to grow cultivars have emerged. They have been crossed within the species, with *Miltoniopsis* and with just about everything else in the *Oncidium* alliance. Although classified as a *Miltonia*, a somewhat different looking plant is *Miltonia warscewiczii* with branched spikes of smaller, waxy, brownish-red or even red flowers. *Odontonia* Debutante (*Miltonia warscewiczii* x *Odontoglossum carniferum*) is an important parent of a number of modern intergeneric hybrids.

OTHER GENERA

There are a number of other genera. The following are horticulturally important either because they are worth cultivating or have been significant in hybridisation.

Aspasia There are about 10 species. *Aspasia principissa* has stalked, compressed pseudobulbs with a pair of leathery leaves. One or more flowers are borne on a spike and are green and white with a large lip. *Aspasia variegata* is somewhat similar. Culture is the same as for Brazilian miltonias, but they are less tolerant of low night temperatures. Subject to this, they are easy to grow and flower. They are important as parents used to impart heat tolerance into their offspring, especially when mated with *Odontoglossum crispum* type flowers.

Brassia There are about 30 species remarkable for the attenuated sepals and petals, giving them the common name of 'spider orchids'. The flowers are mainly in shades of green, brown and white and can be over 20 cm across, often gracefully arranged with many on a long spike. *Brassia verrucosa*, *Brassia gireoudiana* and *Brassia maculata* are some in cultivation. Much used in hybridisation. Cultivation is the same as for cattleyas.

Comparettia These showy orchids are not as commonly cultivated as they should be. They are dwarfish plants with leathery leaves, little in the way of pseudobulbs and numerous thin roots. They are best grown on a slab but otherwise conditions as for Colombian miltonias have produced nice plants. Up to 20 or so 5 cm flowers are borne on a spike, the lip being a prominent feature. *Comparettia falcata* has cerise flowers, *Comparettia coccinea* red flowers and *Comparettia speciosa* a striking orange lip.

Rodriguezia There are about 30 species. The plants are dwarfish, often with small pseudobulbs, and the flowers are borne on graceful arching spikes. *Rodriguezia secunda* can produce several spikes from a single growth, each carrying many 3 cm rose-red flowers. It seems to flower more than once a year. *Rodriguezia venusta (= Rodriguezia bracteata)* is a similar plant, but bears larger fragrant white flowers with a golden disc on the lip. There are varying opinions as to the best way to grow these plants but conditions as for cattleyas are usually successful. Do not over-pot them. They do not like being kept either too dry or too wet for too long and often do best on a slab.

INTERGENERIC HYBRIDS

Some intergeneric hybrids involving odontoglossums were discussed in the previous chapter. Some of the better known remaining ones are listed below. It should be remembered that with so many different species in the ancestry of some of these, and the widely different plant and flower forms used as parents, the intergeneric name itself does not always tell you exactly what to expect.

Aliceara (Brassia x Miltonia x Oncidium) These have produced flowers in spectacular colour combinations. The shape is usually heavily influenced by the *Brassia*, although not so much in some advanced hybrids now appearing.

Brassidium (Brassia x Oncidium) Usually easy to grow and free flowering but the shape is dominated by the *Brassia*.

Miltassia (Miltonia x Brassia) Mostly made with Brazilian miltonias, these are star-shaped flowers but are usually nicely displayed and come in a rainbow of colours.

Miltonidium (Miltonia x Oncidium) These come in all shapes and colours, depending upon the parents.

Rodricidium (Rodriguezia x Oncidium) *Rodricidium* Primi (*Rodriguezia secunda* x *Oncidium sarcodes*) comes with free-blooming coral-red flowers. Widely distributed throughout the world is *Howeara* Mini-Primi (*Rodricidium* Primi x *Leochilus oncidioides*), a charming, multi-spiking miniature.

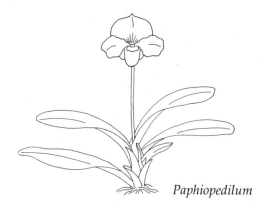

Paphiopedilum

Chapter Fifteen

PAPHIOPEDILUMS

THE PLANT

The lip in *Paphiopedilum* is in the form of a pouch with a fancied resemblance to a slipper, hence the common name of 'slipper orchid'. There is a large prominent dorsal sepal but the other two lower sepals are fused together and usually partially obscured by the pouch. The column is different from any of the other orchids so far discussed in this book, in that there are two anthers with pollinia instead of one and there is a peculiar shield-like structure called the *staminode* protecting the reproductive parts. The plants have thick dark green or mottled leaves, no pseudobulbs and are sympodial in growth habit. The flower stem arises from the growth centre and typically bears a single flower, although there are species which may have more. The flowers are in hues of brown, purple, yellow, green and white. They are popular with florists. They are solid flowers, durable and long lasting when cut and thus suitable for transportation as cut flowers.

Paphiopedilums are usually thought of as terrestrial orchids. In fact they like to grow not in the ground but rather in the organic litter on the forest floor or in rock crevices. There are even a few which grow on tree trunks. The natural geographic range is much the same as for cymbidiums and dendrobiums except that it does not extend as far south as Australia. Paphiopedilums were not so long ago referred to in horticultural circles as cypripediums. However, the true cypripediums, natives of the Northern Hemisphere, are mostly true deciduous terrestrials from higher latitudes and not greenhouse subjects. *Phragmipedium* and *Selenipedium* are two other related genera from tropical America which are occasionally cultivated.

HOUSING

Some of the cooler growing paphiopedilums can be grown in the shadehouse but even these produce better flowers in a greenhouse. Around the world, paphiopedilums are really greenhouse plants. As they have low light requirements many are suitable windowsill subjects, often succeeding in an east or west facing window.

TEMPERATURE

Warm growing kinds and all young seedlings make the best vegetative growth with nightly minimums of 18°C (65°F). The temperature minimums, usually recommended are 15°C to 18°C (60°F to 65°F) for warm growers and 10°C to 15°C (50°F to 60°F) for cool growers. Although in this chapter paphiopedilums have been arbitrarily divided into warm and cool growers, there are many plants with requirements falling somewhere in between and those that are not very fussy about where they are put. It is possible to maintain a mixed collection with night temperatures near the bottom end of the scale with good culture and by not persevering with any plants that do not thrive in this environment. The plants will in any event come to no harm if there are occasional drops in temperature below the minimum if the leaves are dry and the relative humidity is below 100 per cent. In fact some paphiopedilums just must have a nightly drop in temperature to below 15°C (60°F) for two to eight weeks from early autumn to initiate flowers.

Mottled-leaved paphiopedilums are usually warm growers while the cool growers are likely to have green leaves. There are exceptions to this rule so it is not a safe guide. Quite apart from temperature minimums, paphiopedilums, and for that matter all orchids, need to have higher temperatures during daylight hours. Take care to maintain this differential. It will not be a problem in summer when high day temperatures are normal. As to maximum day temperatures, these should ideally not exceed 26°C (80°F) during the growing season and 20°C (68°F) or less during the flowering season. When they cannot be restricted to these figures, maintain relative humidities as high as possible and ensure there is air movement but not a gale.

LIGHT

Paphiopedilums do not like high light intensities. They need less than cattleyas. About 1000 foot-candles is correct, less during the flowering season and possibly a little more in the summer in cool climates or otherwise where air temperatures can be kept within bounds. Too little light will result in fewer flowers. Too much reduces plant size, number of leaves, flower quality and stem length.

WATERING AND NUTRITION

Paphiopedilums should not be allowed to become bone dry at the roots. Water again while the bulk of the growing medium is still just perceptibly moist. Do not let the medium remain continuously wet however. If in doubt, it may be better to water, especially in the summer. When watering be careful not to let water remain in the leaf axils. Nutrients are best added to the water, using the formula recommended for cattleyas. Slow-release materials can be incorporated sparingly in the medium but it may be safer to keep them on the surface.

POTTING

Probably more different recipes for growing media have been used for paphiopedilums than for any other genus. Most modern media are based on bark. Paphiopedilums can be grown in fine bark alone, treated as detailed in Chapter Six. The mix of bark, peat and pumice as given in that chapter for cymbidiums has given better results for some growers. The plants have been grown to perfection in pure sphagnum moss. Paphiopedilums should be repotted into fresh growing medium every two years. If a recipe incorporating a lot of humus (e.g.leaf mold) is used, it may be best to repot annually whether or not the medium has broken down. Paphiopedilums are less resentful of being knocked out of their pots than epiphytes. It is permissible to remove a plant from its pot very occasionally just to examine the root system if you feel something might be wrong there.

The best time to repot is immediately after flowering. Do not over-pot and be careful not to bury the rhizome too low. About 6 mm below the surface of the growing medium is about right. The plants do not have a very extensive root system and if they are not secure stake them until they are established. Large plants can be divided into clumps of not less than three growths.

PROPAGATION

Large plants can be divided as described above. A trick which sometimes works is to sever an old growth from the rest of the plant by cutting the rhizome several months before repotting and leaving it undisturbed. This may induce it to make a new growth from a bud which would otherwise remain dormant. Unfortunately paphiopedilums are reluctant to yield to the tissue-culture process and new, top-quality cultivars tend to be collectors items fetching relatively high prices. Seedlings are raised in large quantities, however, and these are usually a rewarding way of increasing a collection.

PESTS AND DISEASES

Pests are not too troublesome but occasional infestations of scale, mealybug and mites will need to be dealt with. Fungal and bacterial rots are unfortunately more of a problem and can spread with alarming speed. Examine your plants frequently. Cut out decayed areas and adopt the measures suggested in Chapter Eight. Remove dead leaves promptly. Never allow water to accumulate in the leaf axils. If it gets there by accident during watering, apply a preventative wide-spectrum fungicide and then tip the water out, so that any moisture remaining contains the fungicide. If continually troubled by these rots, maintain a coating of protective fungicide on the leaves. Plants housed where the leaves are always dry, the relative humidity never exceeds 90 per cent and there is good air movement are less prone to these diseases. Paphiopedilums otherwise like high humidities so it is necessary to strike a balance.

HYBRIDS AND SPECIES

Many years of hybridising have given us a race of plants with large, long lasting, varnished looking flowers with massive dorsal sepals, wide petals and so-called 'classic' shape. Over more recent years there has been a revival of interest in species fueled by the discovery of a surprising number of new species and the production of different looking primary hybrids. As with some other orchids, the modern hybrids have had any differing cultural requirements in the ancestral species ironed out to a large extent. The grower of species has the challenge of meeting the possibly differing requirements of individual plants to achieve perfection. Only a representative selection from the many species in cultivation is listed below.

Paphiopedilum armeniacum Although first described from China's

Yunnan province as recently as 1982, plants of this species seem to have been suddenly brought into cultivation in unexpectedly large numbers. Its introduction generated much excitement, for nobody had seen anything quite like it. The better forms are quite roundish 8 cm flowers but the salient feature is the all-over deep luminous yellow colour with glowing gold overtones. Appears to flower in winter and spring.

Paphiopedilum bellatulum A small, mottled-leaf plant with 7 cm cream-white flowers spotted reddish-purple. The dorsal sepal and petals are almost round, giving the flower a circular appearance. The flower stem is very short. The species belongs to a group known as brachypetalums. Others in the same group are *P. concolor*, *P. niveum* and possibly *P. armeniacum* and *P. delenatii*. They are all warm growing plants (although *P. bellatulum* may like it marginally cooler) and the growing medium should be allowed to approach dryness (but not dry out) before watering. Keep them in small pots. As they grow in limestone formations, it is common practice to add extra lime to bark-based media. Some growers even incorporate limestone chips or shell grit.

Paphiopedilum callosum Long lasting large flowers are borne on long stems. The green and white flowers are marked with purple lines. Colour is variable and some dark wine-coloured cultivars exist. A vigorous species with mottled leaves. Flowers in late spring and summer. One of the progenitors of the Maudiae-type paphiopedilums.

Paphiopedilum charlesworthii A popular compact cooler growing plant with glossy green leaves. It has a broad rosy-pink dorsal sepal and a relatively small pouch. Autumn flowering.

Paphiopedilum delenatii A smallish plant with mottled leaves marked underneath with purple. The general appearance of the flower is pink. This species is much prized by connoisseurs but has a reputation of being easy to flower but difficult to grow. Some have succeeded with it in pure sphagnum moss. A warm grower, flowering in late spring and summer.

Paphiopedilum fairieanum The dorsal sepals and petals are white but marked with longitudinal stripes which in various forms may be coloured from brown through red to violet or even green in an alba form. The petals curl upward, giving the flower its characteristic appearance. This is a small plant and a cool grower, flowering in winter. It comes from high elevations in the Himalayan foothills, growing on limestone cliffs and subjected to wet summers and dry winters.

Paphiopedilum insigne A cool growing Himalayan species which has a reputation of being easy to grow. It has been widely cultivated for many years by hobbyists and by commercial growers for cut flowers. The plants are variable but typically have 10 cm glossy green flowers. The dorsal sepal is margined in white and spotted red-brown.

Paphiopedilum rothschildianum A relatively large plant with a long flower stem carrying two to five yellowish flowers shaded to white and with almost black stripes on the dorsal and petals. This striking plant is one of the so-called multiflora paphiopedilums. Others in this group include *P. philippinense* and *P. roebelinii*. They are summer flowering. They are warm growing and will take larger pots, more light and more nutrients than other paphiopedilums. They are strong but slow growers and tend to be shy flowerers. Nevertheless they are worth the effort and much sought after by enthusiasts. Some primary hybrids are proving to be easier to flower.

Paphiopedilum sukhakulii A popular warm growing species with mottled leaves. The flowers, borne on long stems, are in shades of green, the flat horizontal petals spotted purple. Flowers autumn through to spring.

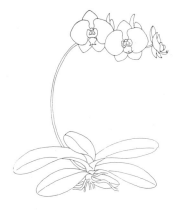

Phalaenopsis

Chapter Sixteen

PHALAENOPSIS

THE PLANT

Phalaenopsis, literally the 'moth orchid', is currently enjoying a surge of popularity. These plants are of increasing importance in the cut-flower trade. Quite large numbers are now grown commercially, the long lasting flowers standing up well to packing and transportation. The beauty and variety in the improved modern hybrids has increased their popularity with hobbyists who have found the plants are relatively easy to grow if given enough warmth. Even a modest collection can have some plants in flower throughout the year. A greenhouse full of flowering *Phalaenopsis* is a breathtaking sight. They can also be grown in the home where they are good windowsill subjects if the room is kept warm.

There are more than 40 species found growing in the wild over a wide area from India in the north down to Queensland. The majority of these orchids are shade-loving plants found growing as epiphytes or lithophytes in warm tropical jungles. There the air is warm most of the time, humidity is high, and it rains frequently. The genus is monopodial in growth habit. There is a single active growing stem, new leaves appearing one atop the other during the life of the plant, that is, unless the growing point is destroyed, in which event a lower node on the stem may break into a new vegetative shoot. The large leathery leaves are deep green or in some species mottled. The flower spike appears from inside one of the upper leaves and may bear from one to 100 flowers, according to the species. Colours range from white and pink to flowers which are blotched, spotted or barred with shades of near red, purple, brown, green and yellow.

The queen of the *Phalaenopsis* is the modern white hybrid which produces an inflorescence of 10 to 20 large (8 cm or more) round, glistening flowers of heavy texture. Some pink hybrids also approach this standard. The hybridisers have worked hard to introduce red, yellow and other colours and good cultivars are keenly sought after. As yet these have not reached the size and shape of the whites. A *Phalaenopsis* can be encouraged to produce a second (or even a third or more in succession) crop of flowers by cutting the flower spike just below the bottom flower rather than at its base. A node on the remaining portion of the spike may then develop and form a new inflorescence. Only a healthy well established plant should be kept in flower in this way.

HOUSING

Phalaenopsis are easiest to grow on their own without the company of other orchids needing different conditions. In a mixed collection it will often be possible to construct a polythene tent at one end of the greenhouse in which the plants can be given the extra warmth and humidity they require. Lining a greenhouse with polythene facilitates the provision of a more humid atmosphere. Ventilate with discretion as the plants do not like draughts of cold air. Nor do they like stagnant air. A fan to circulate inside air is helpful if ventilators cannot be opened. *Phalaenopsis* are popular indoor plants in homes which are kept adequately warm. Relative humidities are often low in a heated home. It helps to place the plants over (not on) a gravel filled tray kept constantly wet. Frequent misting of the plants also helps. When placed on a windowsill, proper shading must of course be provided.

TEMPERATURE

The ideal is to maintain a minimum temperature of 20°C (68°F), especially to keep young seedlings growing. However, adult plants can be maintained with a minimum of 15°C (60°F) if the standard of culture is otherwise good. Night temperatures somewhat below 15°C (60°F) for several weeks in the autumn are actually desirable to encourage some plants to initiate flower spikes. In general, the plants will not be harmed by occasional temperature falls below the minimums mentioned, provided they do not fall too far. Young leaves have been damaged when exposed to 7°C (44°F) for more than four hours. If you are not able to provide the recommended minimum temperatures do not attempt to grow *Phalaenopsis*. On the other hand, it has been shown that merely keeping temperatures at the upper end of the range can compensate for otherwise mediocre culture. Warm daytime temperatures up to 35 °C (95 °F) can be tolerated if humidity is kept high (60 per cent to 70 per cent) and the leaves are kept from overheating.

LIGHT

Less light than cattleyas. About 1000 foot-candles is correct but better to give less in summer than to allow leaves to overheat. Too little light results in soft, fleshy, dark green plants which do not flower. Too much gives stunted yellowish plants with inferior flower quality.

HUMIDITY

Relative humidities over 70 per cent but below 100 per cent are the ideal. Keeping the humidity high on bright summer days is admittedly a problem and a 60 per cent to 70 per cent range is more practicable then. Some suggestions are to be found in Chapter Four. A combination of high light intensity, high air temperatures and low humidity will place severe stress on these plants. Heavily shade during these periods if there is no other control.

WATERING AND NUTRITION

Having no pseudobulbs, the plants have a limited capacity to store water and should not be allowed to remain dry at the roots. Water again before the potting medium has completely dried out and is still perceptibly damp. Nutrients are best supplied in soluble form in the water based on the recommendations for cattleyas. Ensure that water does not remain in the crown of the plant or lie on any part of the leaves for more than an hour or two. Avoid watering the plants with ice-cold water.

POTTING

Plastic pots are usually favoured, but clay ones would be safer for a beginner. Baskets made of wood are safer still. Bark is the most commonly used potting material, using a coarse grade for mature plants. It is used either on its own or with the incorporation variously of polystyrene pieces, charcoal, pumice or sphagnum moss. Incorporate the latter only if your conditions favour a rapid drying cycle. The thick roots have a tendency to wander outside the pot and may resent efforts to coax them back. This is quite natural. Aerial roots should be allowed to remain that way. In nature the plants often grow on a vertical surface, and are inclined so that water drains away from the crown. Hanging baskets off centre or sloping staging can achieve this effect in the greenhouse. Repotting is best done immediately after flowering. Do not over-pot. Rather than subject a mature plant to the shock of being removed from its pot, remove the old medium as best you can (water pressure from a hose is useful) and work new medium around the roots.

PROPAGATION

Occasionally a node on a flower stem will make a vegetative growth which can be removed and potted up when it has made roots. The growth substance benzyl adenine (BA) will encourage this if applied to dormant buds on the older flower spikes. A preparation containing BA is marketed for this purpose. Mericlones of some kinds are offered for sale, as are stem propagations, but the latter are expensive if from superior cultivars. The cheapest way to purchase plants is as seedlings in flasks. If they come from a competent hybridiser who has used top quality plants, the percentage with good quality flowers can be quite high. With optimum growing conditions the largest of the seedlings ex flask could flower within two years.

PESTS AND DISEASES

Control measures are as suggested in Chapter Eight. Rots can spread with alarming rapidity in the succulent leaves and must be dealt with promptly. If a rot develops in the crown (usually the result of stagnant water being allowed to lie there), the death of the plant may follow very quickly. If prompt action does not save the top of the plant, its removal might initiate a secondary growth from the base. Sunken light brown areas (blackening with age) can be symptoms of low temperatures. Any pitting, red or brownish areas, scarring or silvering on either leaf surface should be examined with a hand lens before assuming it is a disease symptom. Very small mites can cause these effects. Slugs, snails and mealybug are other troublesome insect pests.

HYBRIDS AND SPECIES

Most of the *Phalaenopsis* in cultivation now are hybrids. There are intergeneric hybrids but the only one at all common in collections is *Doritaenopsis* (*Phalaenopsis* x *Doritis*). All the modern hybrids will thrive in the same environment. Some species may have their peculiar needs. The few listed below are popular and are a selection from those generally considered not difficult to grow.

Phalaenopsis amabilis White, long lasting flowers up to 10 cm across are borne in profusion on long branching spikes. This widely distributed species grows naturally as far south as Queensland. The modern white tetraploid *Phalaenopsis* is largely founded on this species.

Phalaenopsis equestris The plant has rather thin elongated leaves and a zig-zag flower spike which produces 4 cm-wide white or rose flowers in succession. It is in the background of many candy-striped and red-lipped hybrids.

Phalaenopsis manii A smaller growing plant with star-shaped glossy chestnut-brown flowers barred golden yellow. It seems to tolerate slightly cooler temperatures than other *Phalaenopsis*.

Phalaenopsis stuartiana Long deep green leaves, marbled and barred with silvery-grey and purple beneath, make this an attractive plant. A large branched spike carries many 7 cm glistening white flowers with yellow and red markings in the central parts. In nature this species has the curious ability to produce new plantlets from its roots. It does not seem to do this in cultivation.

Phalaenopsis schilleriana A somewhat similar plant to the one previously described, but the flowers are typically flushed with pink. Both grow naturally in the Phillipines, but whereas the former is found near sea level, this species is commonly found at 1000 m. It has a reputation of being easy to grow and is well worth a place in a mixed collection.

Lycaste

Chapter Seventeen

OTHER GENERA

AERIDES

An Asiatic genus with a monopodial growth habit resembling *Vanda*, to which it is related. Culture is generally the same as for *Vanda sanderiana* (see p.97). Two popular species are *Aerides odoratum* and *Aerides lawrenceae*, which both have pendulous racemes of densely packed waxy flowers (up to 5 cm) shaded and marked with purple. Very fragrant.

ANGRAECUM

Another monopodial genus somewhat similar to *Vanda*, but this one is from Africa and Madagascar. The culture is as for *Vanda sanderiana*, but with a little less light. The large waxy white flowers, often shaded green, have a characteristic long spur at the rear. There are over 200 species, some little known, but *Angraecum eburnum* and *Angraecum sesquipedale*, both quite large plants, have been cultivated for many years. *Angraecum compactum* is a dwarf species which needs more shade and cooler conditions.

ANSELLIA

A sympodial African genus with cane-like cylindrical pseudobulbs up to 50 cm high (usually much shorter), with six or so leaves near the apex.

The flower spike comes from near the top of the cane. The 5 cm flowers come in colours from pure yellow to yellow with red-brown bars. Under some conditions the roots will grow straight up out of the pot like mangrove roots. Ansellias should be potted in media recommended for cattleyas but it is difficult to otherwise suggest specific cultural practices. They have been grown successfully with cattleyas, also with vandas and even with cymbidiums. Possibly much depends upon just where, over its vast geographical range, the particular variety you have came from. Plants cultivated are usually labelled *Ansellia gigantea* or *Ansellia africana* but are probably all forms of the same variable species.

ASCOCENTRUM

An Asiatic genus best described as a smaller edition of *Vanda*, to which it is closely related. Found in collections is *Ascocentrum curvifolium* with 2.5 cm orange flowers on a densely packed straight spike. *Ascocentrum miniatum* has similar coloured flowers but is a dwarf plant which seldom outgrows a 10 cm pot. The important intergeneric hybrid *Ascocenda (Ascocentrum* x *Vanda)* has been developed to combine the best qualities of both genera. They have brightly coloured flowers, including deep blue, on compact plants. The culture of all these is as for *Vanda sanderiana* (see p.97).

BARKERIA

There are 10 species, all native to Central America, and they belong to the *Cattleya* alliance. They have cane-like pseudobulbs from 13 cm to 30 cm high, depending upon the species, and may drop their leaves in the winter. The flowers are inclined to nod, with the sepals and petals held high above the lip in characteristic fashion. Flowers are borne on apical spikes, as in cattleyas, and are mainly in shades of purple, pink and white. All the species are worth cultivating. Grow them as if they were cattleyas but water infrequently in the winter. They have a large, wandering root system for their size and may be better managed on a slab.

CATASETUM

A genus of over 100 species from tropical America. Most species have separate male and female flowers, usually on separate flower spikes and often at different times. Some plants in cultivation seem to produce only male flowers. Green, white and yellow colours predominate. These orchids are an excellent conversation piece. They can be cultivated as if they were cattleyas but prefer a little more warmth and a little more light.

They should be watered with discretion when not in active growth, especially the deciduous kinds. *Cycnoches* and *Mormodes* are closely related genera.

COELOGYNE

Over 100 species grow naturally from the Himalayas down to some Pacific islands. They are sympodial with pseudobulbs, flower spikes often coming from the centre of young growths. Some kinds have long rhizomes and are best grown in a basket. Some are warm growers while others need cool treatment, surviving very low temperatures in winter but needing to be kept cool during hot summers. Potting media and light requirements are very generally as for cattleyas. The cool growers should be kept on the dry side during winter. Some of those popular with growers are listed below.

Coelogyne cristata A decidedly cool grower from high elevations in the Himalayas. Very beautiful snow-white 10 cm flowers are produced in early spring. It can be grown in a shadehouse all year if not likely to be frozen and can be given protection from winter rain. Widely grown in cooler climates.

Coelogyne mooreana Erect flower spikes carry up to eight glistening white 10 cm blooms. Slightly warmer growing than *C. cristata*.

Coelogyne pandurata A much sought-after species with an arching spike of up to 15 large, striking flowers of emerald green with a black lip. A lowland tropical plant which definitely requires warmer treatment.

DISA

A terrestrial genus of over 100 species from South Africa. The most famous is *Disa uniflora* (syn. *Disa grandiflora*) with 10 cm flowers variable in colour but typically vivid scarlet. In nature it likes to grow among ferns and wet mosses below waterfalls or even where it is occasionally submerged in water. After flowering in summer the flowering growth dies but there should be an emerging new growth which will flower the following season. These plants can be grown in a shadehouse with 50 per cent shade the year round if not subjected to other than light frosts, but prefer some shelter such as an unheated greenhouse in the winter. The plants can be grown in pure sphagnum moss. A medium of 25 per cent pumice of 5 mm particle size and 75 per cent sphagnum-moss peat has been used with some success. These plants must not be allowed to dry out at any time. *Disa* can be raised from seed (which does not remain viable for long), employing the techniques used for begonia or fern spores.

LYCASTE

The genus of some 27 species is native to Central and South America. Most of the plants in cultivation are cool growing epiphytes or lithophytes from moderate elevations and flower in the spring. They are sympodial, with broad leaves and oval pseudobulbs. Some, which typically have bright yellow flowers, are deciduous and flower spikes come from the base of the leafless pseudobulbs. Lycastes will usually grow in any medium that is suitable for cymbidiums. They should not be allowed to dry out between waterings in the summer when in active growth but the medium should approach dryness in the winter, especially with the deciduous kinds. Light intensities can be the same as for cattleyas or a little less, not more than 2000 foot-candles. They like cool, airy conditions in summer and a minimum temperature of about 10°C (50°F). They will tolerate occasional falls well below that, but on the other hand do appreciate warmer night temperatures as the new lead is developing. Avoid letting water remain on the leaves at any time as they are very subject to fungal spotting. Some plants in cultivation are:

Lycaste cruenta An epiphyte found growing up to 2200 m. Waxy and fragrant, the long lived flowers are up to 8 cm across, with broad green sepals and yellow or orange petals. Deciduous and spring flowering.

Lycaste deppei An epiphyte or lithophyte with large flowers which are variable, but green sepals, white petals and an orange or yellow lip are typical.

Lycaste skinneri (syn. *Lycaste virginalis)* This *Lycaste* is the national flower of Guatemala and is on the endangered species list. It is certainly not in danger of extinction in cultivation, being one of the most beautiful and most widely grown species in the genus. Some of the better forms in cultivation have, however, been raised from seed. The flowers are variable, but can be up to 15 cm across and pink, although pure-white forms are not uncommon. The plant likes plenty of water and nutrients and not too intense light in the summer. The leaves must be kept cool in summer. Very low winter night temperatures, down to freezing, will be tolerated but not enjoyed. It has been successfully grown with cattleyas.

Hybrids There are many of these, mostly dominated by *Lycaste skinneri* bloodlines. They are plants of great beauty, some of the modern near-red hybrids being outstanding. There are only a few intergenerics, the best known being the yellow *Angulocaste (Anguloa x Lycaste).*

MASDEVALLIA

Over 300 species have been described and at least 100 of these seem to have been in cultivation at one time or another. There are no pseudobulbs, stems with a single fleshy leaf growing from the rhizome in a tufted manner. The flowers arise from the base and are often brilliantly coloured or more sombre with odd or even bizarre shapes. This genus seems to have a compelling fascination for the enthusiasts who collect them. Species are mostly cultivated but an increasing number of hybrids are becoming available. They are usually not large plants and some are miniatures. They are mostly epiphytes from the cloud forests of the Andes. The plants are cool growers. A winter minimum of 10 °C (50 °F) is usually recommended, but it goes much lower in their native habitat and they are good subjects for an unheated greenhouse provided it does not freeze. Masdevallias must be kept cool in the summer and do well in the shadehouse in this season. They do not like high light intensities (not more than 1000 foot-candles in a greenhouse in summer) and should not be allowed to dry at the roots, especially in summer. A growing medium recommended for cattleyas is suitable.

PLEIONE

These are smallish, crocus-like plants sometimes known to alpine specialists as 'Indian crocuses'. Although not taken seriously by some orchid growers for a period, they are becoming popular with the introduction of new species and some hybrids. There has been confusion about the nomenclature and the names on many plant labels may not be what we are told they ought to be. Pleiones are easy to grow by applying a few simple rules. They like plenty of water, warmth and nutrients once in full growth. In winter they are dormant, as by this time the leaves have dropped and they should then be kept dry. It is customary to put a number of bulbs in a shallow pan to make a good display. Pleiones are not too fussy about the growing medium and have even been grown in the garden. They are a good windowsill subject. Most plants in cultivation seem to be *Pleione formosana* or forms of it, spring flowering, with pink or even white flowers some 7 cm across.

RHYNCHOSTYLIS

Monopodial orchids, the plants resemble a smaller edition of a *Vanda*, to which they are related. The flowers are not large but are densely carried in cylindrical racemes. Two popular species are *Rhynchostylis retusa*, with typically white flowers spotted amethyst-purple, and *Rhynchostylis gigantea,* with flowers from white to near red. Culture the same as for *Vanda sanderiana.*

SARCOCHILUS

This is another genus related to *Vanda,* although the plants are much smaller. Two charming spring-flowering species, both native to Australia, are *Sarcochilus falcatus* and *Sarcochilus hartmannii.* The last mentioned has many 2 cm white flowers with reddish markings on the lip and base of the sepals and petals. It is a lithophyte and can be grown in a pot or a basket using medium as for cattleyas. *S. falcatus* is an epiphyte and does not like to have all its roots covered and is best grown in a basket or on a slab. It is known as the 'orange blossom orchid' due to its appearance and fragrance. Both species can be grown under the same conditions as cattleyas but like to be kept cool in summer when they prefer a shadehouse. They should not be allowed to remain dry at the roots for any length of time.

VANDA

There are perhaps 40 *Vanda* species growing from the Himalayas south as far as Queensland. They are monopodial and usually quite large plants with no pseudobulbs but stout stems with short spaces between the leaves which can be strap-like or folded longitudinally into a cylinder. Spikes bearing up to 12 or more flowers come from upper leaf axils. Vandas can be grown in pots but do better in baskets. These are commonly suspended, as the thick fleshy roots like to wander and can be a nuisance on a bench. They can be grown in any medium recommended for cattleyas if into this is incorporated a few larger pieces of bark, polystyrene or charcoal. Water them frequently in summer, using a 100 ppm nitrogen fertiliser. In winter or dull weather they can be dried out but must not be allowed to shrivel. Misting the aerial roots may be sufficient for a day or two if conditions do not favour a full watering. When vandas, after many years, become too tall, the top half of the plant can be severed to make another plant, provided there are a few roots to go with it. The bottom half will often make one or more new shoots in response to this. Otherwise the only method of propagation is by seed, but seedlings are readily available.

Vanda coerulea The famous blue orchid from higher elevations is a cool grower and will tolerate winter temperatures down to 8°C (44°F) or occasionally lower. Some varieties have been nursery raised in the tropics to improve the shape and deep blue colour but have lost this cold tolerance. The plants like strong light, 3000 foot-candles or even more in a shadehouse or greenhouse if leaf temperatures can be kept down and humidity high. Flowers up to 10 cm across appear in autumn and winter.

Vanda sanderiana Sometimes known as *Euanthe sanderiana*, this one comes from the Phillipines. A rounder, flatter and somewhat larger flower than *Vanda coerulea*. The dorsal sepal and petals are pink and the lower sepals have brown tessellations. There is much variation in flower colour and plant breeding has produced some superior strains. Culture is as outlined above, except that minimum night temperatures of 15°C (60°F) are required. It can go a little lower for adult plants but they will make better growth if it is a little higher. Seedlings especially will take many years to reach flowering size if night temperatures are too low. Most of the other species are also warm growers.

Terete vandas These are the ones with the cylindrical leaves. Hybrids based upon them are grown in the tropics, often in full sun, in massive numbers for cut flowers. In climates where they must be grown in a greenhouse it is difficult to give these plants enough light to flower them well. Some semi-terete types (usually hybrids with strap-leaved kinds) may be more manageable. It is better not to attempt to grow too many of these if you live in a cool, temperate climate.

Hybrids A tremendous amount of breeding is being done with vandas, mainly in tropical countries. A range of flowers with classic shapes and a wide range of colours is now available. Although many species have been introduced into the ancestry of these plants, the modern hybrid is heavily based upon *V. coerulea* and *V. sanderiana* bloodlines. The culture of the strap-leaved hybrids is as for *V. sanderiana*.

ZYGOPETALUM

This is a sympodial genus from tropical South America. Commonly found in collections is *Zygopetalum intermedium*, or perhaps *Zygopetalum mackayi*, with green sepals and petals barred red-brown and a broad white lip streaked and spotted with violet-purple. They have pale green glossy pseudobulbs and long narrow leaves. Flower spikes come from the base of the new bulb, with up to ten 8 cm fragrant flowers in winter and spring. These species are usually cultivated as if they were cymbidiums. A few desirable hybrids are appearing, some with rich colours of brown, green and violet.

Appendix

Some Popular Cultivated Common Genera and Intergeneric Hybrids with Standard Abbreviations

ALICEARA (*Alcra.*) — BRASSIA x MILTONIA x ONCIDIUM
ASCOCENDA (*Ascda.*) — ASCOCENTRUM x VANDA
ASCOCENTRUM (*Asctm.*) — Natural genus
ASPASIA (*Asp.*) — Natural genus
ASPOGLOSSUM (*Aspgm.*) — ASPASIA x ODONTOGLOSSUM
BEALLARA (*Bllra.*) — BRASSIA x COCHLIODA x MILTONIA x ODONTOGLOSSUM

BRASSAVOLA (*B.*) — Natural genus
BRASSIA (*Brs.*) — Natural genus
BRASSIDIUM (*Brsdm.*) — BRASSIA x ONCIDIUM
BRASSOCATTLEYA (*Bc.*) — BRASSAVOLA x CATTLEYA
BRASSOLAELIOCATTLEYA (*Blc.*) — BRASSAVOLA x CATTLEYA x LAELIA
BROUGHTONIA (*Bro.*) — Natural genus
CATTLEYA (*C.*) — Natural genus
CATTLEYTONIA (*Ctna.*) — BROUGHTONIA x CATTLEYA
CHARLESWORTHARA (*Cha.*) — COCHLIODA x MILTONIA x ONCIDIUM
COCHLIODA (*Cda.*) — Natural genus
CYMBIDIUM (*Cym.*) — Natural genus
DENDROBIUM (*Den.*) — Natural genus
EPICATTLEYA (*Epc.*) — CATTLEYA x EPIDENDRUM
EPIDENDRUM (*Epi.*) — Natural genus
EPILAELIA (*Epl.*) — EPIDENDRUM x LAELIA
EPITONIA (*Eptn.*) — BROUGHTONIA x EPIDENDRUM
HAWKINSARA (*Hknsa.*) — BROUGHTONIA x LAELIA x CATTLEYA x SOPHRONITIS

HOWEARA (*Hwra.*) — LEOCHILIS x ONCIDIUM x RODRIGUEZIA
LAELIA (*L.*) — Natural genus
LAELIOCATTLEYA (*Lc.*) — CATTLEYA x LAELIA
LOWARA (*Low.*) — BRASSAVOLA x LAELIA x SOPHRONITIS
LYCASTE (*Lyc.*) — Natural genus
MACLELLANARA (*Mclna.*) — BRASSIA x ODONTOGLOSSUM x ONCIDIUM
MASDEVALLIA (*Masd.*) — Natural genus
MILTASSIA (*Mtssa.*) — BRASSIA x MILTONIA
MILTONIA (*Milt.*) — Natural genus
MILTONIDIUM (*Mtdm.*) — MILTONIA x ONCIDIUM
ODONTIODA (*Oda.*) — COCHLIODA x ODONTOGLOSSUM
ODONTOBRASSIA (*Odbrs.*) — BRASSIA x ODONTOGLOSSUM

ODONTOCIDIUM (*Odcdm.*)	ODONTOGLOSSUM x ONCIDIUM
ODONTOGLOSSUM (*Odm.*)	Natural genus
ODONTONIA (*Odtna.*)	MILTONIA x ODONTOGLOSSUM
ONCIDIODA (*Oncda.*)	COCHLIODA x ONCIDIUM
ONCIDIUM (*Onc.*)	Natural genus
PAPHIOPEDILUM (*Paph.*)	Natural genus
PHALAENOPSIS (*Phal.*)	Natural genus
POTINARA (*Pot.*)	BRASSAVOLA x CATTLEYA x LAELIA x SOPHRONITIS
RHYNCHOSTYLIS (*Rhy.*)	Natural genus
RODRICIDIUM (*Rdcm.*)	ONCIDIUM x RODRIGUEZIA
RODRIGUEZIA (*Rdza.*)	Natural genus
SOPHROCATTLEYA (*Sc.*)	CATTLEYA x SOPHRONITIS
SOPHROLAELIA (*Sl.*)	LAELIA x SOPHRONITIS
SOPHROLAELIOCATTLEYA (*Slc.*)	CATTLEYA x LAELIA x SOPHRONITIS
SOPHRONITIS (*Soph.*)	Natural genus
VANDA (*V.*)	Natural genus
VUYLSTEKEARA (*Vuyl.*)	COCHLIODA x MILTONIA x ODONTOGLOSSUM
WILSONARA (*Wils.*)	COCHLIODA x ODONTOGLOSSUM x ONCIDIUM
ZYGOPETALUM (Z.)	Natural genus

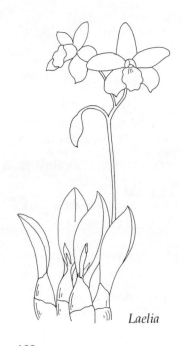

Laelia

Glossary

Aerial root One having no contact with the ground or growing medium.
Air capacity Air-filled pore space.The percentage of the volume of potting medium that contains air after it has been saturated with water and allowed to drain.
Albino An orchid plant lacking the genetic ability to produce red-purple pigments, resulting in only white, green or yellow colour in the flowers.
Backbulb An old leafless pseudobulb.
Chromosomes Bodies which become visible during cell division and are involved in the transmission of hereditary characteristics.
Clone An individual plant raised from a single seed, including any subsequent vegetative propagations.
Column The organ formed by the union of stamens and pistils.
Cross (1) To hybridise. (2) The progeny resulting from hybridisation.
Cultivar In orchids, has almost the same meaning as clone.
Deciduous A plant that sheds its leaves at a certain season.
Diploid Having two sets of chromosomes.
Epiphyte A plant which grows on another plant.
Fertilisation (1)The conversion of ovules into seeds following pollination.(2) The provision of of nutrients for the plant.
Foot-candle A unit of light equivalent to that produced by a candle at a distance of one foot.
Genus A closely related group of plants.
Grex The collective name given to the progeny of parents which are not of the same species or grex.
Hybrid The offspring of a cross between parents that are genetically unlike.
Hybridisation The act of producing hybrids by crossing one species or hybrid with another.
Intergeneric Between or among two or more genera.
Keiki A plantlet produced from the (usually an upper) node of the stem of another plant.
Labellum The third, and usually highly modified, unpaired petal of an orchid flower.
Lead A new vegetative growth.
Lip See labellum.
Lithophyte A plant growing on rocks. Rupicolous.

Mericlone A plant produced in the laboratory by culture of meristematic tissue.

Meristematic Undifferentiated tissue retaining the capacity for further growth, usually found in buds and growing points.

Monopodial A type of plant development in which the terminal bud of the stem continues its vegetative growth indefinitely.

Mycorrhiza A symbiotic relationship between plant roots and fungi.

Node The joint or point on a stem at which a leaf or bract is attached.

Ovary That part of the flower which develops into a seed pod.

Petals The two inner segments of an orchid flower, the third being the lip.

Pod A mature ovary which may contain seed. The fruit of the orchid.

Pollination The act of placing pollen on the stigma.

Pollinia Pollen grains bound together in waxy masses.

Polyploid Having more than two sets of chromosomes — triploid, etc.

Pseudobulb A thickened stem.

Pure colour Australian term referring to an albino cymbidium.

Rhizome The connecting stem between the pseudobulbs or upright growths from which roots are produced.

Seedling A plant raised from seed, particularly a young plant which has yet to flower.

Sepals The three outer segments of the flower and usually the only segments visible in the unopened bud.

Sheath A modified leaf enfolding and protecting new shoots or flower buds.

Species A group of plants (or animals) which may show intergraduation among individual members but having common significant characteristics separating it from any other group.

Spike Used in this book to refer to any type of inflorescence, irrespective of the mode of flower bearing.

Stigma The part which receives the pollen for fertilisation — in orchids usually a sticky cavity found on the undersurface of the column end.

Subtribe One of the natural divisions into which large tribes are sometimes divided.

Symbiosis The living together of dissimilar organisms with benefit to both.

Synonym (syn.) A surplus name, as when a plant has been given two or more names.

Systemic A chemical capable of being absorbed and transported throughout the plant.

Taxonomist A scientist concerned with classification and naming plants and animals.

Terrestrial Growing in or on the ground.

Tetraploid Having four sets of chromosomes.

Tissue culture Growing cells and tissue in an aseptic nutrient medium with the objective of developing whole plants.

Transpiration The loss of water vapour through the leaves.

Tribe A group of related genera forming a natural division within a family.

Triploid Having three sets of chromosomes.

Variety (var.) A population of species found growing in the wild and showing variation from the type species. Only a taxonomist can give a varietal name (which follows the species name and is written in italics).

Vegetative propagation Propagated other than by seed, e.g., by division or tissue culture.

Velamen The layers of spongy cells on the outside of the root.

Virus A sub-microscopic infectious organic particle associated with disease.

Suggested Further Reading

BOOKS

There is an enormous orchid literature. The brief selection below includes books specialising in one subject or one kind of orchid but except where indicated otherwise, they are written to be understood by the ordinary grower.

HAWKES' ENCYCLOPEDIA OF CULTIVATED ORCHIDS

Alex Hawkes. Faber & Faber, 1965
For many years this has been a standard reference book, describing as it does the several thousand species in all genera said to be in cultivation. Only one other book published in modern times attempts to cover this much ground.

THE MANUAL OF CULTIVATED ORCHID SPECIES

Bechtel, Cribb and Launert. Blandford Press, 1986
Contains a description of over 1200 species. Not as many as in the book by Hawkes but over half are illustrated in colour and the work is very authoritative and up-to-date. All species enthusiasts aspire to own either this book or the work by Hawkes.

ORCHIDS. A GOLDEN NATURE GUIDE

Dillon, Zinn and Shuttleworth.
A very popular pocketbook full of realistic paintings of plants and flowers which will enable even the novice to readily identify many of the popular species in cultivation. An inexpensive alternative for those not wishing to purchase either of the two more comprehensive and more expensive books above.

THE PAPHIOPEDILUM GROWERS MANUAL

Lance A. Birk. Pisang Press, 1984
Almost everything the enthusiast would wish to know about this genus is here. Authoritatively written for both the novice and advanced grower. Well illustrated.

TROPICAL ASIATIC SLIPPER ORCHIDS

K.S.Bennett. Salem House, 1985
A cheaper alternative for the grower of paphiopedilums who finds Lance Birk's book a little expensive. Much general information on species and cultural instructions.

BEGINNERS GUIDE TO GROWING PHALAENOPSIS

Bob Gordon.
Just what it says. An inexpensive book for the enthusiast who is a novice but still wants to know more about this genus than is usually found in books on general orchid culture.

HANDBOOK ON ORCHID NOMENCLATURE AND REGISTRATION

The International Orchid Commission.
This relatively inexpensive publication contains the rules for naming orchids. Dry reading for many, but anyone concerned with naming or writing about orchids should have a copy.

THE ORCHIDS. NATURAL HISTORY AND CLASSIFICATION

Robert Dressler. Harvard University Press, 1981
Orchid biology, geography, ecology and evolution, etc. Not necessarily of interest to the novice, but very important because it contains a complete modern revised system of classification of the orchid family.

SANDERS LIST OF ORCHID HYBRIDS

Published by the Royal Horticultural Society for the International Registration Authority
In several volumes covering various periods, this work has already been described on page 12. A reference book for the hybridiser or anyone interested in the parentage of orchid hybrids.

MINIATURE ORCHIDS

Rebecca T. Northen. Van Nostrand Reinhold, 1984
Devoted entirely to the description and cultivation of miniature orchid plants.

HOME ORCHID GROWING

Rebecca T. Northen. Van Nostrand Reinhold, 1971
A comprehensive and ever popular orchid book from the USA, first published in 1950. Includes cultural and other information for a wide range of orchids.

ORCHIDS FOR EVERYONE
By several authors. Hamlyn, 1987
Another general orchid book which includes cultural information for most popular orchids. Written more for conditions in England, but useful anywhere.

PERIODICALS
Orchid societies from many countries publish journals which keep their subscribers informed about what is happening in the orchid world and usually contain articles on a wide range of subjects. Commercial orchid firms advertise their wares in (and often only in) these journals, thus giving the reader interesting information about what plants are being offered for sale, and by whom. A few of these publications, all of which have coloured illustrations, are listed below. Usually one must pay a yearly subscription; copies in your public library will usually yield up-to-date address details.

AMERICAN ORCHID SOCIETY BULLETIN
The American Orchid Society
This journal sets the standard for others. Worldwide membership. Monthly.

AUSTRALIAN ORCHID REVIEW
The Australian Orchid Council
Covers the orchid scene in Australia. Quarterly.

ORCHID ADVOCATE
Official Journal of the Cymbidium Society of America
Published in California but worldwide coverage of developments of interest to all growers of cymbidiums and paphiopedilums. Bi-monthly.

ORCHIDS IN NEW ZEALAND
The Orchid Council of New Zealand
Covers the orchid scene in New Zealand. Bi-monthly.

ORCHID DIGEST
The Orchid Digest Corporation
Published in California. Emphasis is on species; has a reputation for fine colour illustrations. Bi-monthly.

THE ORCHID REVIEW
This journal has been published in England for nearly 100 years. Caters for an international readership at all levels. Monthly.

Approximate Metric Conversions

To convert	to	multiply by
metres (m)	feet	3.28
centimetres (cm)	inches	0.40
millimetres (mm)	inches	0.04
cubic metres (m^3)	cubic yards	1.31
litres (l)	gallons (US)	0.26
litres (l)	gallons (Imp.)	0.22
grams (g)	ounces	0.04
kilograms (kg)	pounds	2.20

Index

Note: **bold** figures refer to coloured photograph numbers